Celebrate!

Woman's Day

Celebrate!

Menus and recipes for joyous feasts

filipacchi
publishing

Filipacchi Publishing
1633 Broadway
New York, NY 10019

© 2003 Filipacchi Publishing
Cover photograph © Alison Miksch

Designed by Patricia Fabricant
Copyedited by Margaret Farley, Greg Robertson and
Kim Walker

ISBN 2-85018-686-4

Printed and bound in Italy

Contents

Holidays are times to celebrate...unless you're the one stuck in the kitchen while your guests are having fun. Wouldn't you like to dazzle everyone with the menu while saving yourself stress over the dishes you're serving? Never fear—*Woman's Day Celebrate!* is here with the perfect menu planners for your Thanksgiving, Christmas and Easter feasts. Find everything from hors d'oeuvres and appetizers to main courses and desserts. These recipes are guaranteed to put a smile on the faces of your family and guests. You'll have a smile on your face, too, thanks to the plan-ahead guides that accompany our complete dinners. No more feeling overwhelmed the day before, and the day of, a big culinary event. We provide a step-by-step count-down for buying, assembling and preparing ahead.

Some recipes can even be started a week in advance, which means more breathing room for you as the big day approaches. Wouldn't you rather be enjoying the "oohs" and "aahs" heard around the table than hearing yourself say "Uh-oh, what did I forget?" With *Celebrate!* in your corner, you won't feel the heat because you'll be out of the kitchen in record time.

And there are more good times to come because *Celebrate!* also includes party treats and tricks for Valentine's Day and Halloween. Show the kids your love by surprising them on February 14 with our Quick-Cut Heart Cookies and Red Velvet Cake. Then give that special someone a slice of your affection with our Sweetheart Cake. On October 31, when the frost's on the pumpkin and there's a chill in the air, bewitch all your ghosts and goblins with devilish delights like Mini-Haunted Houses and our Jack-o'-Lantern Cake. Whatever you decide to serve, you're sure to make any ghoul drool.

No matter what the holiday occasion, we have the menus and recipes that are sure to please you and your guests. And that's definitely something to celebrate!

Thanksgiving Menu for 12

WINTER SQUASH BISQUE

GREEN BEAN & PEA SALAD

GIBLET GRAVY

ROAST TURKEY

NO-COOK CRANBERRY SAUCE

SAUSAGE STUFFING

MASHED CARROTS & RUTABAGA

OYSTER CASSEROLE

CRANBERRY GELATIN MOLD*

APPLE CHEESECAKE IN A GINGERSNAP-WALNUT CRUST

EASY PUMPKIN PIE

*Can be served as a salad or for dessert

Turn to page 24 for our handy Timetable.

Roast Turkey, Giblet Gravy, No-Cook Cranberry Sauce

TIME: About 1 hr 10 min

SERVES 12

PER SERVING (with Garnish):
  218 cal, 4 g pro, 23 g car, 5 g
  fiber, 13 g fat (7 g saturated
  fat), 33 mg chol, 600 mg sod

PLANNING TIP The roasted pepper garnish can be made 1 week ahead. Refrigerate covered. The bisque can be made through Step 2 up to 3 days ahead. Refrigerate covered. About 15 minutes before serving proceed with Step 3. Garnish just before serving.

TIP To peel butternut squash, cut crosswise in thirds, place cut side down on a cutting board and cut off skin with a small paring knife. For acorn squash, use a heavy-duty vegetable peeler, then a paring knife to cut off skin between ridges.

Winter Squash Bisque

1/2 stick (1/4 cup) butter
1 1/3 cups finely chopped onions
1/3 cup finely chopped carrot
3 medium potatoes (1 lb), peeled and cubed (2 1/3 cups)
3 medium acorn squash or butternut squash (4 1/4 lb), halved, seeded, peeled (see Tip) and cubed (9 cups)
6 cups 100% fat-free, reduced-sodium chicken broth
3/4 cup each heavy (whipping) cream and whole milk
1 tsp salt, or to taste
1/2 tsp freshly ground pepper, or to taste
GARNISH: drained roasted red peppers (from 12-oz jar) puréed in a blender with 3 Tbsp olive oil; fresh chives

1 Melt butter in a 4- to 5-qt pot over medium heat. Stir in onions and carrot, cover and cook 6 minutes or until tender. Add potatoes, squash and broth. Bring to a boil, reduce heat, cover and simmer 25 minutes or until vegetables are very soft. Let cool.

2 Process in small batches in a blender or food processor until smooth.

3 Return to pot; stir in cream, milk, salt and pepper. Heat over medium heat.

4 To garnish, drizzle pepper purée on each serving; top with chives.

TIME: About 30 min,
         plus 2 hr chilling

SERVES 12

PER SERVING: 125 cal, 3 g pro,
    19 g car, 3 g fiber, 5 g fat
    (1 g saturated fat), 0 mg chol,
    349 mg sod

PLANNING TIP *The Dressing can be made up to 5 days ahead and the beans cooked 2 days ahead. Refrigerate separately. The bell pepper, onion, celery and pimientos can be cut up to 2 days ahead. Bag pimientos separately, other vegetables together. Refrigerate. The salad can be prepared through Step 3 up to 1 day ahead. To serve, proceed with Step 4.*

TIP *You can substitute cooked frozen whole or cut green beans for the fresh beans.*

Green Bean & Pea Salad

1 lb fresh green beans, ends trimmed (see Tip)
1 bag (1 lb) frozen green peas, thawed
1 yellow bell pepper, seeded and chopped
1 medium onion, halved and thinly sliced
4 ribs celery, chopped
1 jar (4 oz) whole pimientos, drained and sliced

DRESSING
    1/2 cup each sugar and cider vinegar
    1/4 cup oil
    1 1/2 tsp salt
    1/2 tsp freshly ground pepper

Boston lettuce leaves

1 If using fresh beans have ready a large bowl of ice water. Bring 1 in. salted water to a boil in a large skillet or pot. Add beans, cover and steam 5 to 7 minutes until crisp-

tender. Using a slotted spoon, remove to bowl with ice water. Let beans cool, then drain and pat dry with paper towels.

2 Place beans, peas, bell pepper, onion, celery and pimientos in a large bowl.

3 DRESSING: Heat all ingredients over medium-low heat until sugar and salt are dissolved. Let cool. Pour over vegetables and toss gently to mix and coat. Refrigerate at least 2 hours or up to 1 day.

4 Serve on lettuce-lined plates.

Giblet Gravy

Turkey giblets (heart, liver, gizzard), chopped, and turkey neck, left whole (see Step 1 of Roast Turkey recipe, page 14)
2 cans (14 1/2 oz each) 100% fat-free, reduced-sodium chicken broth
1 medium onion, peeled and quartered
1 rib celery with leaves, cut in thirds
1 medium carrot, peeled and cut in thirds
1/2 tsp each salt and freshly ground black pepper
2 cups defatted drippings from Roast Turkey (see recipe, page 14)
1/2 cup each cornstarch and cold water

1 Put giblets and neck in a heavy 3-qt saucepan. Add chicken broth, onion, celery, carrot, salt and pepper, then cool water to cover (pan should be about 3/4 full).

2 Bring to a boil, reduce heat, cover and, stirring occasionally, simmer 4 hours, until broth is flavorful. Pour through a strainer into a 2-qt saucepan (you should have a little over 4 cups). Discard neck. Cover saucepan and refrigerate overnight (see Tip).

3 ABOUT 30 MINUTES BEFORE SERVING: Remove solidified fat from top of gelled broth and add drippings. Bring to a gentle boil. Mix cornstarch and water until smooth. Stir into broth and, stirring gently, cook 4 to 5 minutes until thickened. Remove from heat; cover and let stand until serving.

TIME: About 5 hr

MAKES 6 cups

PER 1/4 CUP: 49 cal, 5 g pro, 4 g car, 0 g fiber, 1 g fat (0 g saturated fat), 32 mg chol, 168 mg sod

PLANNING TIP: The vegetables can be cut up to 3 days ahead. Bag together and refrigerate. Prepare the gravy through Step 2 up to 1 day ahead. Proceed with Step 3 after turkey has roasted and is resting.

TIP While the broth chills, the fat will rise to the top and solidify, making it easy to remove.

About 30 min, plus
3 1/2 to 4 hr roasting
(but see chart,
opposite page)

SERVES 12

PER 4-OZ SERVING (without
skin or stuffing): 231 cal,
32 g pro, 0 g car, 0 g fiber,
11 g fat (3 g saturated fat),
94 mg chol, 115 mg sod

PLANNING TIP *Proceed with
Step 1 up to 1 day ahead.
Return wrapped turkey to
refrigerator. Plan to have the
turkey done about 45 minutes
before serving dinner. Once
cooked, a whole turkey will
stay warm for at least 1 hour.
See Turkey Roasting Chart,
opposite page, for roasting
times.*

TIP *To check temperature in
center of stuffing with a standard meat thermometer (versus instant-read), insert thermometer through body cavity
into stuffing and leave it there
for 5 minutes.*

NOTE *To defat drippings, let
fat rise to the top, then spoon
it off.*

Roast Turkey

1 whole turkey (12 to 14 lb), fresh or frozen, thawed
Sausage Stuffing (see recipe, page 16)
1 Tbsp butter, melted
1/2 tsp each salt and pepper
1 cup 100% fat-free, reduced-sodium chicken broth
GARNISH: fresh herbs, orange slices and red currants

1 Remove giblets, neck and any fat from turkey body
and neck cavities. Reserve giblets and neck for Giblet
Gravy (recipe, page 13); discard fat.

2 Heat oven to 325°F. Have ready a shallow roasting
pan with rack. Dry turkey inside and out with paper towels.
Lightly spoon some stuffing into neck cavity. Fold skin flap
under back; fasten with skewers or toothpicks. Loosely stuff
body. Tie or clamp legs together. Twist wing tips under
back. Brush skin with butter; sprinkle with salt and pepper.

3 Place breast side up on rack in pan. Insert standard
meat thermometer (if not using instant-read) into center of
a thigh next to body (not touching bone). Add broth to pan.

4 Roast 3 1/2 to 4 hours, basting every 30 minutes
with pan juices, adding more broth or water if pan seems
dry. If breast gets too brown, cover loosely with foil.

5 About 2/3 through roasting time, untie drumsticks so
heat can penetrate body.

6 About 1 hour before turkey should be done, start
checking for doneness. When thermometer reads 180°F in
thigh and center of stuffing registers 165°F (see Tip), remove
turkey to a serving platter or carving board. Let rest about
30 to 45 minutes for juicier meat and easier carving.

7 While the turkey rests, pour drippings into a 4-cup
measure; remove fat from drippings (see Note). Reserve 2
cups defatted drippings for Giblet Gravy (recipe, page 13).
Garnish turkey platter before serving.

TURKEY ROASTING CHART

Because turkey body shapes differ, these cooking times are approximate. The times are based on open-pan roasting of a chilled turkey (with a starting internal temperature of 40°F) in a 325°F oven.

WEIGHT (lb)	UNSTUFFED (hr)	STUFFED (hr)
8 to 12	2 3/4 to 3	3 to 3 1/2
12 to 14	3 to 3 3/4	3 1/2 to 4
14 to 18	3 3/4 to 4 1/4	4 to 4 1/4
18 to 20	4 1/4 to 4 1/2	4 1/4 to 4 3/4
20 to 24	4 1/2 to 5	4 3/4 to 5 1/4

Roasting times based on recommendations from the U.S. Department of Agriculture.

No-Cook Cranberry Sauce

1 bag (12 oz) cranberries, picked over
1/2 orange, cut up (with peel), seeds removed
1/2 apple, cored, cut up (with peel)
3/4 cup sugar, or to taste

Put all ingredients in a food processor and pulse until fruit is finely chopped. Makes 2 3/4 cups.

TIME: About 10 min

SERVES 12

PER SERVING: 68 cal, 0 g pro, 18 g car, 1 g fiber, 0 g fat (0 g saturated fat), 0 mg chol, 1 mg sod

PLANNING TIP *Can be made up to 2 days ahead. Refrigerate in covered serving bowl.*

TIME: About 1 hr 15 min

MAKES 18 cups

PER 1/2 CUP: 95 cal, 4 g pro,
14 g car, 1 g fiber, 3 g fat
(1 g saturated fat), 7 mg chol,
294 mg sod

PLANNING TIP The bread can be torn up to 3 days ahead. Store airtight at room temperature. Chop onions and celery up to 2 days ahead; bag together and refrigerate. Cook sausage, bag and refrigerate up to 1 day ahead. Mix stuffing just before using.

TIP Even if you stuff the bird, you'll have extra stuffing. Spoon it into a greased shallow baking dish, drizzle with 1/2 cup broth, cover tightly with foil and bake 30 minutes in a 350°F oven. Uncover and bake 15 minutes longer until top is lightly toasted.

Sausage Stuffing

1 tube (12 oz) reduced-fat pork sausage, thawed if frozen
1 loaf (2 lb) firm white sandwich-style bread
2 cups chopped onions
1 1/2 cups chopped celery with leaves
1 1/2 Tbsp poultry seasoning
1 tsp each salt and freshly ground black pepper
1 can (14 1/2 oz) 100% fat-free, reduced-sodium chicken broth
GARNISH: celery leaves

1 Cook sausage in a large nonstick skillet over medium-high heat, breaking up chunks with a wooden spoon, 7 minutes or until no longer pink. Remove to paper towels to drain and cool.

2 Tear bread in pieces into a very large bowl or pot. Add sausage, onions, celery, poultry seasoning, salt and pepper; stir to mix well. Gradually add broth, tossing stuffing until evenly moistened.

3 Lightly stuff neck and body cavities of turkey; bake rest of stuffing separately (see Tip) in a 325°F oven.

Mashed Carrots & Rutabaga

2 lb carrots, peeled and cut in 1/2-in.-thick rounds (5 cups)
One 2-lb rutabaga (see FYI, opposite page), peeled and cut in
   3/4-in. cubes (6 cups)
1/2 stick (1/4 cup) butter
1 1/2 tsp salt
1/2 tsp freshly ground black pepper
1/4 cup chopped fresh dill

1 Put carrots and rutabaga in a 5- to 6-qt pot; add water to cover. Bring to a boil, reduce heat, cover and boil gently 25 to 30 minutes until very tender.

2 Drain in a colander, return to pot, add butter, salt and pepper, and mash until just in small pieces, not smooth. Stir in dill. Transfer to a microwave-safe serving dish, cover and refrigerate up to 1 day.

3 To SERVE: Heat in microwave, stirring once or twice.

TIME: About 1 hr

SERVES 12

PER SERVING: 86 cal, 2 g pro, 12 g car, 4 g fiber, 4 g fat (2 g saturated fat), 10 mg chol, 366 mg sod

PLANNING TIP *Peel and cut the carrots and rutabaga up to 3 days ahead. Bag together and refrigerate. Cook and mash up to 1 day ahead. Spoon into microwave-safe serving dish, cover and refrigerate. Reheat in microwave.*

FYI *Rutabagas are sometimes called wax turnips because they're often coated with wax to preserve freshness. They're also called yellow turnips, Swedes or Swedish turnips.*

CLOCKWISE FROM TOP LEFT: *Sausage Stuffing, Mashed Carrots & Rutabaga, Oyster casserole.*

SERVES 12

PER SERVING: 214 cal, 6 g pro, 17 g car, 1 g fiber, 14 g fat (8 g saturated fat), 78 mg chol, 376 mg sod

PLANNING TIP *Shucked oysters are perishable and should be purchased no more than 2 days before using. The saltines can be crushed, bagged and kept at room temperature up to 1 week. The bell pepper and scallions can be cut, bagged and refrigerated up to 2 days before using. The casserole can be assembled through Step 3 up to 4 hours before baking.*

TIP *Shucked oysters can be bought in vacuum cans or freshly shucked in their liquor (juice). They should smell fresh and briny and the liquor should be viscous and clear, not cloudy.*

Oyster Casserole

1 pt shucked oysters (halved, if large), in their liquor
About 1 cup (1/2 pt) heavy (whipping) cream
1 large egg
1 can (8 3/4 oz) whole kernel corn, drained
1 can (8 1/4 oz) cream-style corn
1 1/2 cups fine saltine cracker crumbs (from 44 finely crushed saltines)
1/2 cup each finely diced red bell pepper and thinly sliced scallions
1/2 stick (4 Tbsp) butter, melted
1/4 tsp salt
1/8 tsp freshly ground black pepper

1 Lightly coat a 2-qt shallow baking dish with nonstick spray.

2 Drain liquor from oysters into a 2-cup glass measure. Add enough cream to make 1 cup. Whisk in egg until well blended.

3 Put whole and cream-style corn in a large bowl. Add cream mixture, 1 1/4 cups cracker crumbs (put remaining 1/4 cup in a small bowl), the bell pepper, scallions, 3 Tbsp butter, the salt and pepper. Stir to mix well. Gently stir in oysters. Pour into prepared baking dish. Stir remaining 1 Tbsp butter into remaining 1/4 cup cracker crumbs to moisten. Sprinkle around edges of casserole. Cover and refrigerate up to 4 hours.

4 Heat oven to 325°F. Uncover casserole and bake 1 hour or until set and crumb topping is lightly browned.

Cranberry Gelatin Mold

1 pkg (6 oz) strawberry-flavor gelatin
2 cups boiling water
1 can (16 oz) whole-berry cranberry sauce
1 can (15 1/4 oz) crushed pineapple in juice
1 can (11 oz) mandarin orange segments, drained
1/2 cup chopped walnuts
GARNISH: mandarin orange segments and mint sprig

1 Rinse a 10-cup mold or fluted tube pan with cold water. Have ready a large bowl half-filled with ice and water.

2 Put gelatin in a medium metal bowl, add the boiling water and stir 2 minutes or until gelatin completely dissolves.

3 Stir cranberry sauce in the can to break it up. Stir into gelatin. Add pineapple and its juice, the orange segments and nuts. Set metal bowl into bowl with ice water; stir until mixture is consistency of unbeaten egg whites. Pour into mold, cover and refrigerate until firm enough to unmold, 24 hours or up to 3 days.

4 UP TO 5 HOURS BEFORE SERVING: Dip mold up to rim in warm, not hot, water about 10 seconds. Tip mold to check that gelatin is released. Invert serving plate over mold. Invert mold and plate together and shake gently from side to side until gelatin drops from mold. Repeat if necessary.

5 Refrigerate until serving. Garnish with orange segments and mint sprig.

TIME: About 35 min,
        plus 24 hr chilling

SERVES 12

PER SERVING: 177 cal, 2 g pro, 37 g car, 1 g fiber, 3 g fat (0 g saturated fat), 0 mg chol, 57 mg sod

PLANNING TIP *Can be made through Step 3 up to 3 days ahead. Leave in mold, cover and refrigerate. Unmold onto a serving platter up to 5 hours before serving. Refrigerate. Garnish just before serving.*

TIME: About 2 hr 20 min, plus at least 4 hr chilling

SERVES 12

PER SERVING: 466 cal, 12 g pro, 46 g car, 1 g fiber, 27 g fat (14 g saturated fat), 116 mg chol, 392 mg sod

PLANNING TIP *Can be made through Step 6 up to 3 days ahead. Proceed with Step 7 up to 1 hour before serving.*

NOTE *To toast walnuts, spread in baking pan and bake at 325°F, stirring once, 10 to 15 minutes.*

Apple Cheesecake in a Gingersnap-Walnut Crust

CRUST

- 20 gingersnap cookies
- 1/2 cup walnuts, toasted (see Note), cooled
- 2 Tbsp each *melted stick butter and sugar*

FILLING

- 2 Tbsp stick butter
- 3 Golden Delicious apples (1 1/4 lb) peeled, halved, cored and cut in 1/2-in. chunks
- 1 cup plus 2 Tbsp sugar
- 3 bricks (8 oz each) 1/3-less-fat cream cheese (Neufchâtel), softened
- 1 Tbsp cornstarch
- 3 large eggs, at room temperature
- 1/4 cup apple-flavored brandy (Applejack or Calvados) or apple cider

TOPPING
1 tub (16 oz) reduced-fat sour cream
1/4 cup sugar

GARNISH: *finely chopped walnuts and thin apple wedges (see Tip)*

1 Heat oven to 325°F. Coat a 9-in. springform pan with nonstick spray.

2 CRUST: Place ingredients in a food processor; pulse until fine crumbs form, then press firmly over bottom of pan. Or put gingersnaps and walnuts in a heavy-duty ziptop bag; crush to fine crumbs with a rolling pin. Transfer to prepared pan. Stir in butter and sugar until blended; press crumbs firmly over bottom of pan.

3 FILLING: Melt butter in a large nonstick skillet over medium heat. Add apples and, stirring occasionally, cook 13 minutes or until pale brown. Stir in 2 Tbsp sugar and cook, stirring often, 5 minutes longer until apples are golden brown (be careful they don't burn). Transfer to a plate. Beat cream cheese, remaining 1 cup sugar and the cornstarch in a large bowl with mixer on medium speed until smooth, scraping sides and bottom of bowl as needed. Beat in eggs 1 at a time just until blended. Reduce speed to low; beat in brandy and apples just to mix. Pour over Crust.

4 Bake 50 to 55 minutes until edges puff slightly and center still jiggles when shaken. Remove from oven.

5 TOPPING: Mix ingredients in a small bowl. Pour evenly over filling; smooth surface. Bake 5 minutes.

6 Place pan on a wire rack. Carefully run a thin knife around edge of cake to release. Cool completely in pan. Cover pan with plastic wrap. Refrigerate at least 4 hours or up to 3 days.

7 UP TO 1 HOUR BEFORE SERVING: Remove pan sides. Place cake on a serving plate. Garnish with walnuts and apple wedges.

TIP *To keep the apple wedges from discoloring, dip them in lemon juice and dry on paper towels.*

TIME: About 50 min,
plus 24 hr chilling

SERVES 8 (see Tip)

PER SERVING: 482 cal, 2 g pro,
51 g car, 1 g fiber, 30 g fat
(16 g saturated fat), 71 mg
chol, 264 mg sod

TIP For 12 to 16 servings, make
2 pies.

Easy Pumpkin Pie

CRUST & DECORATIONS
*1 box (15 oz) refrigerated ready-to-bake pie crust
  (2-crust package)
White from 1 large egg mixed with 1 Tbsp water
3 whole cloves*

FILLING
*4 1/2 cups fresh miniature marshmallows
1 1/2 cups canned 100% pure pumpkin
1 1/2 tsp pumpkin pie spice
1/8 tsp salt
1 1/2 cups heavy (whipping) cream*

GARNISH: *whipped heavy cream*

1 Heat oven to 450°F. Have ready a 9-in. pie plate, a 1 1/2-in. leaf-shape cookie cutter and 2 wooden skewers. Lightly coat a baking sheet with nonstick spray.

2 CRUST: Line pie plate with 1 pie crust; brush with some of the egg white mixture. Flute or crimp edges. Bake crust as package directs. Cool shell before filling.

3 MEANWHILE MAKE DECORATIONS: Unfold remaining pie crust. PUMPKINS: Divide 1/4 the circle into 3 equal pieces. Roll each piece into a ball. Insert a clove pointed end up in top of each for a stem. Press back of a knife lengthwise in 5 or 6 places around pumpkins to form sections. Place on prepared baking sheet. LEAVES: With cookie cutter cut out 12 leaves from 1/2 circle of remaining dough. Place 1 in. apart on baking sheet. VINES: Cut four long 1/8-in.-thick strips from remaining dough. Lightly coat wooden skewers with nonstick spray. Loosely coil strips around skewers; place skewers on baking sheet.

4 Brush pumpkins and leaves with egg white mixture. Bake vines 4 minutes, leaves 5 minutes and pumpkins 10 minutes, removing them from the oven to a wire rack as they brown. Let cool completely on rack.

PLANNING TIP *The baked crust and decorations can be stored airtight at cool room temperature up to 5 days. The pie can be filled, covered and refrigerated up to 3 days. Garnish just before serving.*

5 FILLING: Put ingredients, except cream, in a 3-qt saucepan. Stir over low heat 4 to 5 minutes until marshmallows melt and mixture is smooth. Let cool.

6 Beat cream in a large bowl with mixer on high speed until soft peaks form when beaters are lifted. Fold into pumpkin mixture. Pour into pie shell. Cover and refrigerate until firm enough to cut, 24 hours or up to 3 days.

7 JUST BEFORE SERVING: Garnish with whipped cream, pumpkins, leaves and vines.

Thanksgiving Dinner Timetable

THREE TO FOUR WEEKS AHEAD
- Make guest list. Extend invitations.
- Check supply of chairs, dishes, glasses and utensils, and arrange to borrow or rent what you don't have.

TWO WEEKS AHEAD
- Order turkey to be sure you get the size you want. Check that it fits in your refrigerator and oven.
- Make shopping list. Shop for nonperishable food.
- Plan table settings and centerpiece.

ONE WEEK AHEAD
- Pick up turkey if frozen.
- Get out china, serving dishes and serving utensils. Polish silver if necessary.
- Crush saltine crackers for Oyster Casserole. Store at room temperature.
- Make Pepper Purée garnish for Winter Squash Bisque. Refrigerate covered.

SATURDAY BEFORE THANKSGIVING
- Bake pie crust and decorations for Easy Pumpkin Pie. Store airtight at room temperature.
- Prepare Dressing for the Green Bean & Pea Salad. Cool; refrigerate covered.

MONDAY BEFORE THANKSGIVING
- Shop for perishable food.
- Put frozen turkey in refrigerator to thaw.
- Make Winter Squash Bisque through Step 2. Refrigerate.
- Prepare onion, celery and carrot for Giblet Gravy. Bag together; refrigerate.
- Tear bread for Sausage Stuffing; bag. Store at room temperature.

- Cut vegetables for Mashed Carrots & Rutabaga. Bag together; refrigerate.
- Make Cranberry Gelatin Mold through Step 3. Refrigerate in covered mold.
- Make Apple Cheesecake in a Gingersnap-Walnut Crust through Step 6. Refrigerate in pan.
- Prepare filling and fill crust for Easy Pumpkin Pie. Cover and refrigerate.

TUESDAY BEFORE THANKSGIVING
- Purchase oysters for Oyster Casserole. Refrigerate.
- Cut bell pepper and scallions for Oyster Casserole. Bag together; refrigerate.
- Cut bell pepper, onion, celery and pimientos for Green Bean & Pea Salad. Bag pimientos separately; bag other vegetables together. Refrigerate all.
- Chop onions and celery for Sausage Stuffing. Bag together; refrigerate.
- Prepare green beans for Green Bean & Pea Salad through Step 1. Bag; refrigerate.
- Make No-Cook Cranberry Sauce. Refrigerate in serving dish.
- Start making extra ice.

DAY BEFORE THANKSGIVING
- Buy flowers or centerpiece.
- Pick up turkey if fresh. Prepare Roast Turkey through Step 1. Refrigerate.
- Prepare Green Bean & Pea Salad through Step 3. Refrigerate.
- Prepare Giblet Gravy through Step 2. Refrigerate.
- Prepare sausage for Sausage Stuffing, through Step 1. Bag and refrigerate.
- Cook and prepare Mashed Carrots & Rutabaga. Refrigerate in microwave-safe serving dish.
- Set table.
- Chill beverages.

THANKSGIVING MORNING

- *Finish making stuffing.*
- *Stuff turkey. Spoon extra stuffing into baking dish. Cover and refrigerate.*
- *Start roasting 12- to 14-lb turkey so it will be done 45 minutes before dinner. Check the Turkey Roasting Chart, page 15, for roasting time if turkey is smaller or larger.*

ABOUT 5 HOURS BEFORE DINNER

- *Assemble Oyster Casserole. Cover and refrigerate.*
- *Unmold Cranberry Gelatin Mold on serving platter. Refrigerate.*
- *Prepare garnishes for turkey platter, Cranberry Gelatin Mold and Apple Cheesecake.*

ABOUT 2 HOURS BEFORE DINNER

- *Start checking turkey for doneness.*

1 HOUR BEFORE DINNER

- *Bring Mashed Carrots & Rutabaga to room temperature.*
- *Bring garnish for Winter Squash Bisque to room temperature.*
- *Transfer turkey to serving platter. Cover with foil.*
- *Put covered refrigerated stuffing in baking dish in oven.*
- *Place uncovered Oyster Casserole in oven.*
- *Remove pan sides from Apple Cheesecake. Place on serving plate.*
- *Whip cream to garnish Easy Pumpkin Pie. Cover and refrigerate.*

30 MINUTES BEFORE DINNER

- *Finish making Giblet Gravy.*
- *Garnish Cranberry Gelatin Mold. Refrigerate until serving.*

15 MINUTES BEFORE DINNER

- *Finish cooking Winter Squash Bisque.*
- *Heat Mashed Carrots & Rutabaga in microwave.*
- *Line plates with lettuce for Green Bean & Pea Salad; add salad.*
- *Garnish turkey platter.*

JUST BEFORE SERVING

- *Ladle Winter Squash Bisque into soup plates and garnish.*
- *Pour Giblet Gravy into gravy boat.*
- *Set out No-Cook Cranberry Sauce.*

JUST BEFORE SERVING DESSERTS

- *Garnish Easy Pumpkin Pie and Apple Cheesecake.*

EXPAND YOUR FRIDGE SPACE

- *Make meals that don't have leftovers and use up any leftovers you do have.*
- *Check labels of open jars and bottles to see if contents need to be refrigerated. Many don't.*
- *Pack nonfragile foods in sturdy ziptop bags. Squeeze out air, then seal and press food flat so bags can be stacked.*
- *Use a picnic cooler and frozen ice packs to store condiments, sauces and anything that may not be used daily.*
- *Top food dishes with baking sheets so you can place more food on top.*

Thanksgiving Menu for 12

CHEESE TORTE

FALL SPINACH SALAD

SPICY SESAME ANGEL BISCUITS

ROAST TURKEY WITH ROASTED MINI-PUMPKINS

EVERYTHING STUFFING

MAKE-AHEAD TURKEY GRAVY

MASHED POTATOES WITH BROWNED ONIONS

SQUASH & GREENS GRATIN

GREEN BEANS WITH TOMATO-OLIVE BUTTER

CRANBERRY SAUCE

CRANBERRY, APPLE & ORANGE GELATIN MOLD

APPLE-CRANBERRY CAKE WITH CIDER SAUCE

PUMPKIN FLANS

GINGERBREAD COOKIES

Turn to page 44 for our handy Timetable.

*Roast Turkey with Roasted Mini-Pumpkins and Make-Ahead
Turkey Gravy, Cranberry Sauce, Everything Stuffing*

TIME: 15 min, plus at least
24 hr chilling
DECORATE: Depends on skill

SERVES 12

PER SERVING: 258 cal, 12 g pro,
8 g car, 1 g fiber, 20 g fat
(12 g saturated fat), 53 mg
chol, 378 mg sod

PLANNING TIP *The pine nuts can be toasted up to 1 week ahead. The recipe can be made through Step 2 up to 3 days ahead; bring to room temperature before serving. Ingredients for Turkey Garnish can be prepared a day ahead.*

TOASTING NUTS AND SESAME SEEDS

Put nuts or seeds in a medium skillet over medium heat. Stirring often, cook 3 to 4 minutes or until fragrant and lightly browned. Cool completely.

Cheese Torte

1 log (11 oz) goat cheese, crumbled
2 bricks (8 oz each) 1/3-less-fat cream cheese (Neufchâtel)
1/2 cup crumbled feta cheese
2 Tbsp purchased pesto sauce (jar or tub)
1/2 cup golden raisins, chopped
1/3 cup sundried tomatoes, chopped
1/3 cup pine nuts (pignoli), toasted (see Toasting Nuts, left)
TURKEY GARNISH: parsley leaves, thyme and rosemary sprigs, sage leaves, pumpkin seeds and roasted red pepper
ACCOMPANIMENTS: sliced Italian bread and long, thin breadsticks

1 Line a 9-in. springform pan with plastic wrap, letting wrap extend over sides. Stir all 3 cheeses in a large bowl until blended. Divide mixture in half.

2 Spoon half into prepared pan; spread evenly. Top with pesto, then sprinkle with half the raisins, half the tomatoes and half the pine nuts. Spoon on remaining cheese; spread evenly. Sprinkle with remaining tomatoes, raisins and pine nuts. Cover with overhanging plastic wrap and refrigerate at least 24 hours.

3 Uncover, then invert serving plate on pan. Invert pan and plate together. Remove pan and plastic wrap. Arrange garnish ingredients to resemble a turkey (see photo, opposite page). Serve with accompaniments.

TIME: 25 min

SERVES 12

PER SERVING: 241 cal, 4 g pro,
  14 g car, 3 g fiber, 21 g fat
  (3 g saturated fat), 0 mg chol,
  190 mg sod

PLANNING TIP *Walnuts can be toasted and dressing made up to 1 week ahead. Store nuts at room temperature; refrigerate dressing. Prepare oranges and remove seeds from pomegranate up to 2 days ahead. Wash spinach up to 1 day ahead. Bag each separately and refrigerate. Avocados can be sliced up to 3 hours before using. Toss with lemon juice to prevent discoloring.*

TIP *To remove pomegranate seeds, cut off bud end and score rind from top to bottom in a few places. Immerse fruit in water 5 minutes, then, under water, break sections apart and separate seeds from membranes. Discard membranes; drain seeds.*

Fall Spinach Salad

DRESSING
  3 Tbsp each orange juice and white-wine vinegar
  1/2 cup olive oil
  2 Tbsp Dijon mustard
  1 shallot or white part of 3 scallions, minced
  1/2 tsp salt
  1/4 tsp pepper

15 cups loosely packed spinach leaves (from two 10-oz bags), torn in bite-size pieces (about 15 oz)
2 avocados, peeled, pitted and sliced
4 navel oranges, peeled, white part (pith) removed and sectioned
1 cup walnut pieces, toasted (see Toasting Nuts, page 28)
Seeds from 1 pomegranate (see Tip)

1 Put Dressing ingredients in a small bowl or jar with tight-fitting lid. Whisk or shake until blended.

2 TO SERVE: Toss spinach and 1/2 cup Dressing in a large serving bowl. Add avocados, oranges and walnuts; toss gently to mix. Arrange on plates; sprinkle with pomegranate seeds. Serve remaining dressing on the side.

Spicy Sesame Angel Biscuits

1 pkt (2 1/4 tsp) active dry yeast
1/2 cup warm water (105° to 115°F)
1 1/2 cups buttermilk, at room temperature
5 cups flour
3/4 cup grated Parmesan cheese
1/3 cup sesame seeds, toasted (see Toasting Nuts, page 28)
2 Tbsp sugar
1 Tbsp baking powder
1 tsp each baking soda and salt

1/2 tsp ground red pepper (cayenne)
1/4 tsp ground black pepper
1 stick (1/2 cup) cold butter, cut up
1/2 cup solid vegetable shortening

1 Have baking sheet(s) ready. Stir yeast and warm water in a medium bowl until yeast dissolves. Stir in buttermilk.

2 TO MAKE DOUGH IN FOOD PROCESSOR: Process flour, cheese, sesame seeds, sugar, baking powder, baking soda, salt, and red and black pepper until blended. Add butter and shortening; pulse until mixture resembles coarse crumbs. Transfer to a large bowl. Add yeast mixture; stir just until a soft dough forms. BY HAND: In a large bowl, stir flour, cheese, sesame seeds, sugar, baking powder, baking soda, salt, and red and black pepper until blended. Add butter and shortening, in small pieces. Cut in with a pastry blender until mixture resembles coarse crumbs. Add yeast mixture; stir just until a soft dough forms.

3 Turn dough out onto a lightly floured surface and knead gently about 15 times until smooth and elastic. With a floured rolling pin, roll out dough to a 12-in. square. Cut in six 2-in.-wide strips. Cut each strip diagonally crosswise to make 7 diamond-shaped biscuits. Prick tops with a fork. Place 1 1/2 in. apart on ungreased baking sheets, cover with a towel and let rise 45 minutes (dough won't rise much).

4 Heat oven to 400°F. Bake 1 sheet at a time 15 minutes or until biscuits are browned. Remove to wire rack to cool.

TIME: 1 hr 35 min (includes baking 2 batches)

MAKES 42

PER BISCUIT: 116 cal, 3 g pro, 13 g car, 1 g fiber, 6 g fat (2 g saturated fat), 7 mg chol, 179 mg sod

PLANNING TIP *Bake up to 3 weeks ahead. Cool, store airtight and freeze. Bring to room temperature before serving.*

TIP *When cutting the dough, flour the knife between each cut.*

TIME: 30 min, plus 4 hr
        roasting (but see
        chart, page 15)

SERVES 12

PER 4-OZ SERVING (without
  skin or stuffing): 231 cal,
  32 g pro, 0 g car, 0 g fiber,
  11 g fat (3 g saturated fat),
  94 mg chol, 115 mg sod

TIP *To check temperature in
center of stuffing with a standard meat thermometer (versus
instant-read), insert thermometer through body cavity and
leave it there 5 minutes.*

ROASTED MINI-PUMPKINS

*Cut the tops off edible mini-
pumpkins such as Sweet Dump-
ling, Jack-Be-Little or Golden
Nugget. Scrape out seeds and
stringy pulp. Brush inside and
out with melted butter, sprinkle
with salt, pepper and sage or
other dried herb. Roast on a
baking sheet in 400°F oven 30
to 40 minutes until tender. Serve
warm or at room temperature.*

PLANNING TIP *Pumpkins can
be made up to 1 day ahead.
Refrigerate covered.*

Roast Turkey with Roasted Mini-Pumpkins

1 whole turkey (12 to 14 lb), fresh or frozen, thawed
Everything Stuffing (see recipe, opposite page)
1 Tbsp butter, melted
1/2 tsp each salt and pepper
1 cup 100% fat-free, reduced-sodium chicken broth
*GARNISH: Roasted Mini-Pumpkins (see directions, left) and
  fresh herbs*

1 Heat oven to 325°F. Have ready a shallow roasting pan with rack. Remove giblets, neck and any fat from turkey body and neck cavities. Discard giblets and neck or reserve for another use. Discard fat. Dry turkey inside and out with paper towels.

2 Lightly spoon some stuffing into neck cavity. Fold skin flap under back; fasten with skewers or toothpicks. Loosely stuff body. Tie or clamp legs together. Twist wing tips under back. Brush skin with butter; sprinkle with salt and pepper.

3 Place breast side up on rack in pan. Insert standard meat thermometer (if not using instant-read) into center of thigh next to body (not touching bone). Add broth to pan.

4 Roast 3 1/2 to 4 hours, basting every 30 minutes with pan juices, adding more broth or water if the pan seems dry. If breast gets too brown, cover loosely with foil.

5 About 2/3 through roasting time, untie drumsticks so heat can penetrate into body cavity.

6 About 1 hour before turkey should be done, start checking for doneness. When thermometer reads 180°F in thigh and center of stuffing registers 165°F (see Tip), remove turkey to a serving platter or carving board. Let rest about 30 to 45 minutes for juicier meat and easier carving. Garnish platter before serving.

Everything Stuffing

1 bag (14 oz) cubed herb stuffing
1 bag (7 oz) cornbread stuffing
1 lb sweet Italian sausage, casing removed
3/4 stick (6 Tbsp) butter or margarine
2 cups chopped onions
2 Golden Delicious apples, peeled, cored and coarsely chopped
1 cup chopped celery
8 oz crimini or white mushrooms, sliced
8 oz shiitake mushrooms, stemmed, sliced
1/4 tsp each salt and pepper
1/2 cup chopped parsley
2 Tbsp minced fresh sage or 2 tsp dried
1 jar (7.4 oz) unsweetened whole, dry chestnuts, broken in
   large pieces
2 cans (about 14 oz each) chicken broth

1 Combine stuffing mixes in a large bowl. Brown sausage in a large skillet over medium-high heat 10 minutes, stirring to break up chunks. Transfer with slotted spoon to stuffing mixes. Pour off all but 2 Tbsp drippings from skillet. Add 2 Tbsp butter, the onions, apples and celery; sauté 8 minutes or until tender. Add to bowl with stuffing mixture.

2 Melt remaining 4 Tbsp butter in skillet; add mushrooms, salt and pepper and cook 5 minutes until softened. Add to bowl along with parsley, sage and chestnuts. Gradually add broth; toss until evenly moistened. Stuff neck and body of turkey; bake the rest (see Tip).

TIME: 1 hr 35 min (includes
         time in baking dish)

MAKES 18 cups

PER 1/2 CUP: 137 cal, 4 g pro,
   17 g car, 1 g fiber, 6 g fat
   (2 g saturated fat), 13 mg
   chol, 440 mg sod

PLANNING TIP *Up to 3 days ahead, chop onions, apples, celery and parsley; slice mushrooms; and mince fresh sage. Wrap parsley and sage separately in damp paper towels. Refrigerate with onions, apples and celery. Bag and refrigerate mushrooms separately. Make stuffing 1 day ahead, bag and refrigerate, but don't stuff the bird until just before roasting.*

TIP *Even if you stuff the bird, you'll have extra stuffing. Spoon it into a greased baking dish, drizzle with 1/2 cup broth, cover and bake 30 minutes in a 325°F oven. Uncover and bake 15 minutes longer until top is browned.*

PLANNING TIP *Make up to 3 months ahead; freeze in an air-tight container. Thaw 2 days in refrigerator. Reheat in saucepan, whisking often (see Tip).*

TIP *On Thanksgiving, after the turkey is cooked and removed from the roasting pan, you can skim the fat off the pan drip-pings and add the drippings to the heated gravy.*

Make-Ahead Turkey Gravy

4 turkey wings (about 3 lb)
2 medium onions, peeled and quartered
1 cup water
8 cups chicken broth
3/4 cup chopped carrot
1/2 tsp dried thyme
3/4 cup flour
2 Tbsp stick butter
1/2 tsp freshly ground pepper

1 Heat oven to 400°F. Have ready a large roasting pan.

2 Arrange wings in a single layer in pan; scatter onions over top. Roast 1 1/4 hours until wings are browned.

3 Put wings and onions in a 5- to 6-qt pot. Add water to roasting pan and stir to scrape up any brown bits on bottom. Add to pot. Add 6 cups broth (refrigerate remaining 2 cups), carrot and thyme. Bring to a boil, reduce heat and simmer, uncovered, 1 1/2 hours.

4 Remove wings to cutting board. When cool, pull off skin and meat. Discard skin; save meat for another use.

5 Strain broth into a 3-qt saucepan, pressing vegetables to extract as much liquid as possible. Discard vegetables; skim fat off broth and discard. (If time permits, refrigerate broth overnight to make fat-skimming easier.)

6 Whisk flour into remaining 2 cups broth until blended and smooth.

7 Bring broth in saucepan to a gentle boil. Whisk in broth-flour mixture and boil 3 to 4 minutes to thicken gravy and remove floury taste. Stir in butter and pepper. Serve or pour into containers; refrigerate up to 1 week or freeze up to 3 months.

Mashed Potatoes with
Browned Onions

3/4 stick (6 Tbsp) butter
4 large sweet onions (about 2 3/4 lb), halved lengthwise
    and thinly sliced
1 Tbsp cider vinegar
4 1/2 lb baking (russet) potatoes, peeled and quartered
1 1/2 cups 1% lowfat milk
2 1/2 tsp salt
3/4 tsp freshly ground pepper

1 Melt butter in a large wide-bottom pot or large, deep
skillet over medium-low heat. Add onions; stir to coat.
Cover and cook 10 minutes or until onions are softened
and exude liquid. Uncover, increase heat to medium-high
and cook about 20 minutes longer, stirring often, until
onions are very soft, golden brown and reduced to 2 3/4
cups. Stir in vinegar; remove to a bowl.

2 Meanwhile, in another large pot, cook potatoes in
water to cover 15 to 20 minutes until tender when pierced.
Reserve 1/2 cup cooking water; drain potatoes. Heat milk in
a saucepan or microwave until hot.

3 Return hot potatoes to pot. Mash with handheld mixer
on medium speed or potato masher until smooth. Gradually
beat or mash in hot milk, salt and pepper until potatoes are
smooth and fluffy, gradually adding reserved cooking water if
needed. Stir in onions, reserving some for garnish.

TIME: 1 hr

SERVES 12

PER SERVING: 230 cal, 6 g pro,
    39 g car, 4 g fiber, 6 g fat
    (4 g saturated fat), 17 mg chol,
    582 mg sod

PLANNING TIP The onions can
be cooked up to 3 days ahead.
Bag and refrigerate. Bring to
room temperature before using.
Mashed potatoes can be made
up to 1 day ahead, spooned
into a casserole, covered and
refrigerated. Reheat, covered, in
a 350°F oven 25 to 30 minutes,
or microwave. (If a bit dry, stir
in some milk.)

TIME: 1 hr 45 min

SERVES 12

PER SERVING: 172 cal, 8 g pro,
19 g car, 4 g fiber, 8 g fat
(5 g saturated fat), 23 mg chol,
330 mg sod

PLANNING TIP *Prepare through
Step 3. Cool, cover and refrigerate up to 2 days. Bring to room
temperature before reheating.*

TIP *Use a combination of
squash for different colors and
shapes, and microwave just
until soft enough to cut easily.*

CLOCKWISE FROM TOP: *Mashed
Potatoes with Browned Onions,
Squash & Greens Gratin,
Green Beans with Tomato-
Olive Butter*

Squash & Greens Gratin

3 lb butternut, acorn and/or buttercup squash (see Tip)
*3 leeks (1 1/2 lb), white and pale-green parts only, halved
   lengthwise, then sliced crosswise*
1/2 tsp salt
1/4 tsp pepper
2 Tbsp stick butter
3 large carrots, thinly sliced
1 box (10 oz) frozen chopped kale, thawed and squeezed dry
1 1/2 cups (about 6 oz) shredded Gruyère or Swiss cheese
1/2 cup grated Parmesan cheese
1 cup chicken broth

1 Heat oven to 375°F. Grease a shallow 2 1/2- to 3-qt
baking dish. Halve squashes (see Tip), scoop out seeds
and peel. Cut in 1/2-in.-thick slices.

2 Rinse leeks in a colander; let drain. Mix salt and pepper in a cup. Heat butter in a large skillet over medium
heat; add leeks and 1/4 tsp salt mixture. Cook 5 minutes
until soft. Stir in carrots; cook 5 minutes longer.

3 Arrange 1/3 the squash in prepared baking dish; sprinkle with 1/3 the remaining salt mixture. Top with half the
kale, half the Gruyère cheese, half the carrot mixture, and 3
Tbsp Parmesan cheese. Repeat layers once. Top with remaining squash. Pour broth over all and sprinkle with remaining
salt mixture. Cover with foil and bake 45 minutes.

4 Uncover, sprinkle with remaining Parmesan cheese
and bake 15 minutes longer or until vegetables are tender.
Let stand 15 minutes before serving.

TIME: 25 min

SERVES 12

PER SERVING: 76 cal, 2 g pro,
  8 g car, 2 g fiber, 5 g fat
  (2 g saturated fat), 10 mg chol,
  155 mg sod

PLANNING TIP *Can be pre-
pared through Step 2 up to 2
days ahead. Refrigerate beans
in a plastic ziptop bag and butter mixture covered. Seed and
dice tomato up to 1 day ahead;
refrigerate covered.*

TIP *If you aren't cooking the
beans ahead, cook as directed
in Step 1 for 7 to 9 minutes,
drain, toss with the butter mixture and serve.*

TIME: 40 min

MAKES 5 cups

PER 1/4 CUP: 102 cal, 0 g pro,
  22 g car, 1 g fiber, 0 g fat
  (0 g saturated fat), 0 mg chol,
  2 mg sod

PLANNING TIP *Can be made
up to 2 weeks ahead. Refrigerate airtight.*

Green Beans with Tomato-Olive Butter

3 lb green beans, trimmed

TOMATO-OLIVE BUTTER
  1/2 stick (1/4 cup) butter, softened
  1/4 cup kalamata olives, pitted and finely chopped
  1 Tbsp tomato paste
  1 tsp freshly grated lemon peel
  1/4 tsp salt
  1/8 tsp pepper

1 small tomato, seeded and diced

1 Add beans to a large pot of boiling water and cook 4 minutes or until crisp-tender. Drain in a colander; rinse under running cold water until cold. Pat dry with paper towels.

2 Mix Tomato-Olive Butter ingredients in a small bowl until blended.

3 To SERVE: Bring 1/2 cup water to boil in a large skillet or pot. Add beans and cook 4 minutes or until hot and water evaporates. Remove from heat, add butter mixture and toss until melted. Transfer to serving bowl; sprinkle with tomato.

Cranberry Sauce

1 3/4 cups sugar
2 cups dry red wine
2 bags (12 oz each) fresh cranberries, picked over and rinsed
1/4 cup balsamic vinegar

Bring all ingredients to boil in a large saucepan. Reduce heat and simmer uncovered 20 minutes or until thickened. Pour into serving bowl, cool, cover and refrigerate.

Cranberry, Apple & Orange Gelatin Mold

1 box (8-serving size) orange-flavor gelatin

2 1/4 cups water

3/4 cup orange juice

1/2 cup dried cranberries

1 small Golden Delicious apple, peeled, quartered and cored; 1/2 thinly sliced, the other 1/2 diced

1/2 cup pecans, toasted (see Toasting Nuts, page 28) and chopped

GARNISH: fresh kumquats

1 Have ready a 5- to 6-cup mold or tube pan.

2 Put gelatin in a medium bowl. Bring water just to a boil. Add to gelatin; stir until completely dissolved. Stir in orange juice.

3 Refrigerate until gelatin is consistency of unbeaten egg whites (see Tip). Fold in cranberries, apple and nuts.

4 Rinse mold with cold water, pour in gelatin mixture, cover and refrigerate at least 8 hours until firm, or up to 3 days.

5 To UNMOLD: Run a knife around edge of mold. Dip mold up to rim in warm, not hot, water about 5 seconds. Moisten serving plate with cold water (if gelatin lands off-center you can slide it to the middle). Tip mold to check that gelatin is released. Invert serving plate over mold. Invert mold and plate together and shake gently from side to side until gelatin drops onto plate. Remove mold; garnish with kumquats. Refrigerate until serving.

TIME: 45 min, plus at least 8 hr chilling

SERVES 12

PER SERVING: 111 cal, 2 g pro, 20 g car, 1 g fiber, 3 g fat (0 g saturated fat), 0 mg chol, 36 mg sod

PLANNING TIP *The pecans can be toasted up to 1 week ahead. The gelatin can be made through Step 4 up to 3 days ahead. Cover and refrigerate in mold.*

TIP *For speedy gelling, set bowl of dissolved gelatin in a larger bowl half-filled with ice and water. Stir with a rubber spatula until consistency of unbeaten egg whites. Remove from ice water and stir in solid ingredients.*

TIME: 1 hr 55 min or
       2 hr 5 min (see Tip)

SERVES 12

PER SERVING (without sauce):
365 cal, 5 g pro, 51 g car, 2 g
fiber, 16 g fat (9 g saturated
fat), 72 mg chol, 361 mg sod

PLANNING TIP *The baked
cake can be kept covered at
room temperature up to 3
days or wrapped airtight and
frozen up to 1 month. Thaw
in wrapping at room temperature 1 day ahead.*

TIP *The size of the springform
pan determines the baking
time. Baking will take longer in
a 9-in. pan than a 10-in. one
since the batter will be deeper.*

Apple-Cranberry Cake with Cider Sauce

2 1/4 cups flour
1 1/2 tsp ground cinnamon
1 tsp baking powder
1/2 tsp each baking soda and salt
1 1/2 sticks (3/4 cup) butter, softened
3/4 cup sugar
1/3 cup packed brown sugar
2 large eggs
1 cup buttermilk
*2 Granny Smith apples, peeled, cored and
   diced in 1/2-in. pieces*
1/2 cup dried cranberries, coarsely chopped

TOPPING
   1/4 cup granulated sugar
   3 Tbsp flour
   2 Tbsp cold stick butter, cut up
   1/4 tsp each ground cinnamon and ginger
   1/4 cup pecans, chopped

Cider Sauce (see recipe, opposite page)

1 Heat oven to 350°F. Grease and flour a 9- or 10-in.
springform pan. In a medium bowl, stir flour, cinnamon,
baking powder, baking soda and salt until blended.

2 Beat butter in a large bowl with mixer on medium
speed until creamy. Gradually add sugars; beat 2 minutes
or until fluffy. Beat in eggs 1 at a time until well blended.
On low speed, alternately beat in flour mixture and buttermilk, beginning and ending with flour mixture. Reserve 1/2
cup diced apples and 2 Tbsp chopped cranberries. Stir
remaining apples and cranberries into batter and spread
evenly in prepared springform pan.

3 TOPPING: Put sugar, flour, butter, cinnamon and ginger in a medium bowl. Mix with fingers until crumbly. Stir in pecans and reserved apple and cranberries; sprinkle on batter.

4 Bake 1 hour 15 minutes to 1 hour 25 minutes (see Tip, opposite page) or until a wooden pick inserted in the center of the cake comes out clean. Let cool in pan on a wire rack before removing pan sides. Serve with Cider Sauce.

CIDER SAUCE

2 cups apple cider
1/3 cup light corn syrup
3 Tbsp light-brown sugar
2 Tbsp fresh lemon juice
2 Tbsp stick butter, softened
1 tsp cornstarch
1/8 tsp ground cinnamon

Stir cider, syrup, sugar and lemon juice in a medium saucepan until blended. Bring to a boil, reduce heat slightly and boil gently 15 minutes or until reduced to 1 1/3 cups.

Meanwhile stir butter, cornstarch and cinnamon in a cup until smooth. Reduce heat to low under cider mixture; whisk in butter mixture. Simmer 1 minute or until slightly thickened. Serve warm or at room temperature.

TIME: 30 min

SERVES 12

PER SERVING: 76 cal, 0 g pro, 15 g car, 0 g fiber, 2 g fat (1 g saturated fat), 5 mg chol, 33 mg sod

PLANNING TIP *Can be prepared 1 week ahead. Cover and refrigerate. Bring to room temperature or reheat to serve.*

Pumpkin Flans

1 1/2 cups sugar
4 large eggs
1 cup canned pumpkin purée
1 can (5 oz) evaporated milk (not sweetened condensed)
1/3 cup 1% lowfat milk
3/4 tsp pumpkin pie spice
1 tsp grated orange peel
Gingerbread Cookies (see recipe, opposite page)

1 Put 1 oven rack in center of oven. Heat to 325°F. Have ready six 6-oz ramekins or custard cups and a shallow roasting pan.

2 Cook 1 cup sugar (see Note) in a medium saucepan over medium heat, swirling pan occasionally, until sugar melts and turns amber brown. Immediately pour into ramekins. Holding ramekins with a potholder, tilt so syrup coats bottoms and halfway up sides. Let syrup cool.

3 In a large bowl whisk eggs until blended. Add remaining 1/2 cup sugar, pumpkin, evaporated milk, lowfat milk, spice and orange peel; whisk just until blended. Pour into ramekins.

4 Place 5 ramekins in roasting pan, leaving space for last ramekin. Place pan on center oven rack. Pour hot tap water into open space in pan to come halfway up sides of ramekins. Place last ramekin in pan.

5 Bake 50 minutes or until a thin knife inserted in centers comes out clean. Carefully remove ramekins to a wire rack to cool completely. Cover loosely and refrigerate at least 8 hours.

6 TO SERVE: Run a thin, sharp knife around sides of ramekins. Place inverted serving plates over ramekins and invert. Leave ramekins inverted a few minutes so syrup can run onto plate. Serve with Gingerbread Cookies.

Gingerbread Cookies

1 box (14 oz) gingerbread cake and cookie mix

DECORATING ICING
   1 1/2 cups confectioners' sugar
   1 1/2 Tbsp milk

1 Heat oven to 375°F. Have baking sheet(s) ready.

2 Prepare cake mix to make cookies as directed on package. Cut out with 2- to 3-in. leaf and/or pumpkin cookie cutters. Place 1 in. apart on ungreased baking sheet(s) and bake as directed. Remove to wire racks to cool.

3 TO DECORATE: Mix sugar and milk in a small bowl until smooth. Spoon into a qt-size ziptop bag, snip tip off bottom corner of bag and squeeze icing through opening to decorate cookies. Let icing dry overnight. Serve with Pumpkin Flans (see recipe, opposite page).

TIME (without decoration): 40 min (for baking 3 batches)

MAKES about 52

PER 2 COOKIES: 44 cal, 0 g pro, 9 g car, 0 g fiber, 1 g fat (0 g saturated fat), 1 mg chol, 59 mg sod

PLANNING TIP *Can be baked up to 1 month ahead and frozen. Decorate up to 3 days ahead and store loosely covered at room temperature.*

Thanksgiving Dinner Timetable

THREE TO FOUR WEEKS AHEAD

- Make guest list. Mail invitations or telephone guests.
- Check supply of chairs, dishes, glasses and utensils, and arrange to borrow or rent what you don't have.
- Bake Apple-Cranberry Cake. When cool, wrap airtight and freeze.
- Bake Spicy Sesame Angel Biscuits. Cool, bag airtight and freeze.
- Bake Gingerbread Cookies (don't decorate). Cool, bag airtight and freeze.
- Prepare Make-Ahead Turkey Gravy. Freeze in airtight container.

TWO WEEKS AHEAD

- Order turkey to be sure you get the size you want. Check that it fits in your refrigerator and oven.
- Make shopping list. Shop for nonperishable food.
- Plan table settings.
- Prepare Cranberry Sauce. Refrigerate in an airtight container.

ONE WEEK AHEAD

- Make dressing for Fall Spinach Salad. Refrigerate tightly covered.
- Toast the pine nuts for Cheese Torte, the walnuts for Fall Spinach Salad and the pecans for Cranberry, Apple & Orange Gelatin Mold. Wrap separately; store at room temperature.
- Make Cider Sauce for Apple-Cranberry Cake. Cover and refrigerate.

SATURDAY BEFORE THANKSGIVING

- Pick up turkey if frozen.
- Get out china, serving dishes and serving utensils. Polish silver if necessary.

MONDAY BEFORE THANKSGIVING

- Shop for perishable food.
- Put frozen turkey in refrigerator to thaw.
- Prepare Cheese Torte through Step 2. Cover and refrigerate.
- Chop onions, apples, celery and parsley; slice mushrooms; and mince fresh sage for Everything Stuffing. Wrap parsley and sage separately in damp paper towels. Refrigerate in bag with onions, apples and celery. Bag and refrigerate mushrooms separately.
- Cook onions for Mashed Potatoes with Browned Onions. Bag and refrigerate.
- Make Cranberry, Apple & Orange Gelatin Mold through Step 4. Refrigerate in mold.
- Make Pumpkin Flans through Step 5. Cool, cover and refrigerate in ramekins.
- Thaw Gingerbread Cookies, then decorate. Store loosely covered at room temperature.

TUESDAY BEFORE THANKSGIVING

- Transfer Make-Ahead Turkey Gravy from freezer to refrigerator to thaw.
- Prepare oranges and pomegranate seeds for Fall Spinach Salad. Bag separately and refrigerate.
- Prepare Squash & Greens Gratin through Step 3. Cool, cover and refrigerate.
- Prepare Green Beans with Tomato-Olive Butter through Step 2. Bag beans, cover Tomato-Olive Butter and refrigerate.
- Start making extra ice.

DAY BEFORE THANKSGIVING

- Buy flowers.
- Pick up turkey if fresh. Refrigerate.
- Remove Apple-Cranberry Cake from freezer, if frozen. Thaw in wrapping at room temperature.
- Prepare Everything Stuffing. Bag and refrigerate.
- Wash and bag spinach for Fall Spinach Salad. Refrigerate.
- Roast Mini-Pumpkins; refrigerate loosely covered.

- Prepare Mashed Potatoes with Browned Onions. Refrigerate in covered baking dish.
- Prepare herbs and other ingredients for Turkey Garnish on Cheese Torte.
- Prepare tomato for Tomato-Olive Butter. Refrigerate covered.
- Transfer Cranberry Sauce to serving bowl. Refrigerate covered.
- Set table.
- Chill beverages.

THANKSGIVING MORNING
- Remove Spicy Sesame Angel Biscuits from freezer. Thaw on baking sheet at room temperature.
- Remove Roasted Mini-Pumpkins from refrigerator. Let come to room temperature.
- Stuff turkey. Spoon extra stuffing into baking dish, cover and refrigerate.
- Start roasting 12- to 14-lb turkey so it will be done 45 minutes before dinner. Check the Turkey Roasting Chart, page 15, for roasting time if turkey is smaller or larger.

3 HOURS BEFORE DINNER
- Bring covered Cheese Torte to room temperature.
- Arrange Gingerbread Cookies on serving plate.
- Unmold Cranberry, Apple & Orange Gelatin Mold onto serving platter. Garnish and refrigerate.
- Unmold Pumpkin Flans. Refrigerate.
- Prepare avocado for Fall Spinach Salad. Toss with lemon juice to coat to prevent discoloring.

ABOUT 2 HOURS BEFORE DINNER
- Start checking turkey for doneness.
- Bring Cider Sauce to room temperature, if not heating.
- Bring Squash & Greens Gratin to room temperature.
- Invert Cheese Torte onto serving plate. Garnish as instructed. Leave at room temperature. Slice Italian bread accompaniment and set out breadsticks. Cover until guests arrive.

- Put refrigerated stuffing in baking dish in oven with turkey 30 minutes before turkey will be done.
- Bring Tomato-Olive Butter to room temperature.
- Fill creamers for coffee and refrigerate.

45 MINUTES BEFORE DINNER
- Transfer turkey to serving platter. Cover lightly with foil.
- Uncover stuffing in baking dish; bake 15 minutes longer until browned.

30 MINUTES BEFORE DINNER
- Remove stuffing from oven. Cover to keep hot.
- Divide oven in thirds and increase heat to 350°F. Put covered Mashed Potatoes with Browned Onions on lower shelf. Uncover Squash & Greens Gratin, sprinkle with cheese and put on upper shelf.

15 MINUTES BEFORE DINNER
- Heat Make-Ahead Turkey Gravy. Add turkey drippings, if desired.
- Remove Squash & Greens Gratin from oven.
- Finish cooking Green Beans with Tomato-Olive Butter.
- Prepare Fall Spinach Salad.

JUST BEFORE SERVING
- Garnish turkey platter.
- Put food into serving dishes and set out.
- Pour gravy into gravy boat.

10 MINUTES BEFORE SERVING DESSERT
- If desired, heat Cider Sauce.

Christmas Buffet Menu

Christmas Cheese Spread

Pork Loin with Prunes, Port and Apples

Garlic Mashed Potatoes with Kale

Potato-Pear Gratin

Stuffed Turkey Breast

Fruited White and Wild Rice Salad

Christmas Salad

Lemon-Poached Pears with Two Sauces

Cranberry-Chocolate Trifle

Yule Log

CLOCKWISE FROM TOP LEFT: *Potato-Pear Gratin, Fruited White and Wild Rice Salad, Stuffed Turkey Breast with Lime-Cilantro Sauce*

MAKES 2 1/4 CUPS

PER 3 TBSP: 113 cal, 5 g pro, 1 g car, 0 g fiber, 10 g fat (6 g saturated fat), 33 mg chol, 239 mg sod

PLANNING TIP You can make this spread at least 1 day or up to 1 week ahead. The tree garnish can be made 1 day ahead. Refrigerate parsley and tomato in plastic bags with a moist paper towel, and roasted red pepper and carrot stars and ribbons in ice water.

PITA CHIPS

Split 8 mini pita pockets to get 2 rounds each. Cut each round in 4 wedges. Place cut side up on 2 rimmed baking sheets. Spray with nonstick cooking spray; sprinkle with ground cumin. Bake in 400°F oven 8 to 12 minutes until crisp and lightly browned around edges. Cool, then store airtight at room temperature up to 2 days. Makes 64 chips.

Christmas Cheese Spread

GARLIC-HERB SPREAD

2 bricks (8 oz each) 1/3-less-fat cream cheese (Neufchâtel), cut in cubes

3 oz feta cheese, crumbled (2/3 cup)

2 Tbsp fresh oregano leaves or 2 tsp dried, crumbled

1 tsp minced garlic

TREE GARNISH: parsley leaves, bottled roasted red peppers, large carrot, cherry tomato

ACCOMPANIMENTS: Pita Chips (see recipe, left), assorted crackers and breadsticks

1 Line a 9-in. pie plate with plastic wrap. In food processor, process spread ingredients until smooth. Spread evenly in lined pie plate. Cover with plastic wrap placed directly on surface. Refrigerate at least 24 hours until firm enough to unmold.

2 TO UNMOLD: Uncover pie plate. Place serving plate on top and invert platter and pie plate together. Uncover spread and smooth surface with a spatula.

3 TREE GARNISH: Arrange parsley leaves on spread in shape of Christmas tree. Cut 1 large and several small stars from roasted peppers (1 1/2-in. and 3/4-in. cookie cutters work well). Cut 3/4-in. stars from carrot slices. Using vegetable peeler, peel 2 long carrot "ribbons." Cut both in half lengthwise; place in ice water to curl. Cut cherry tomato in half, trim top third off 1 half for "pot." Serve with accompaniments.

TIME: About 1 hr 50 min

SERVES 8

PER SERVING (with 1/2 apple):
504 cal, 50 g pro,
30 g car, 3 g fiber, 20 g fat
(8 g saturated fat),
144 mg chol, 670 mg sod

PLANNING TIP *Place Savory Baked Apples in oven 45 minutes before roast is done.*

TIP *Have your butcher crack the pork roast's chine (backbone) and, for an elegant presentation, french the ribs (trim meat from ends of bones).*

NOTE *After the bones are frenched, the roast will weigh 4 1/2 to 5 lb.*

SAVORY BAKED APPLES

Cut 2 large Granny Smith and 2 Rome Beauty apples in half from top to bottom. Scoop out core (a melon baller works well). Place cut side down in shallow baking dish. Pour on 3/4 cup chicken broth, dot with 2 Tbsp butter and sprinkle with pepper. Bake alongside pork 20 minutes. Turn apples cut side up, baste with pan juices and bake 15 to 20 minutes longer until tender.

Pork Loin with Prunes, Port and Apples

1 Tbsp minced garlic
1 1/2 tsp grated lemon peel
1 Tbsp chopped fresh sage or 1 tsp dried
1/2 tsp each salt and pepper
5 1/2-lb pork loin roast, excess fat trimmed (see Tip and Note)
2 1/2 cups chicken broth
1/2 cup Ruby port wine or chicken broth
2 Tbsp cornstarch
15 large prunes, cut in quarters
1 Tbsp honey
ACCOMPANIMENT: Savory Baked Apples (see recipe, left)
GARNISH: sage sprigs

1 Place oven rack in lowest position. Heat to 350°F. Have ready a shallow roasting pan with rack.

2 Mix garlic, lemon peel, sage, salt and pepper. Cut about twelve 1/2-in.-wide, 1/2-in.-deep slits into rounded side of pork. Press some garlic mixture into slits; rub remaining over roast.

3 Place the pork, bones up, on rack in roasting pan.

4 Roast 1 hr 20 min to 1 hr 40 min (18 to 20 min per lb) or until a meat thermometer inserted into center of meat not touching bone reads 155°F for medium, 165°F for well-done (temperature will rise about 5°F while standing). Place on large serving platter; cover loosely with foil.

5 Pour fat and drippings in pan into a small bowl or 1-cup glass measure. Let stand until fat rises to top. Skim off fat; reserve drippings.

6 Place pan on 2 burners over medium heat. Add 2 1/4 cups of the broth, the wine and reserved drippings. Stir, scraping up browned bits on bottom of pan. Whisk cornstarch into remaining 1/4 cup broth; add to pan with prunes and honey. Bring to boil, reduce heat and simmer,

stirring occasionally, until prunes get plump and gravy thickens slightly, about 5 minutes.

7 To SERVE: Garnish platter with sage. Cut roast between rib bones. Serve with Savory Baked Apples.

Time: 30 min

Serves 8

Per serving: 280 cal,
  8 g pro, 43 g car, 6 g fiber,
  10 g fat (6 g saturated fat),
  25 mg chol, 572 mg sod

PLANNING TIP *Prepare through Step 2 up to 2 days ahead. Refrigerate covered. To serve, add kale and heat on stovetop or in microwave, stirring occasionally and adding more milk as needed.*

TIP *If you prefer to use fresh kale instead of frozen, trim 1 lb and discard base and tough ribs. Cut crosswise in strips and steam 5 to 10 minutes or until tender.*

Garlic Mashed Potatoes with Kale

4 lb baking potatoes, scrubbed, cut in 1-in. chunks
6 cloves garlic
1 3/4 cups 1% lowfat milk
6 Tbsp butter or margarine, cut in small pieces
1 1/2 tsp salt
3/4 tsp pepper
1 pkg (10 oz) frozen chopped kale, thawed and squeezed dry

1 Cook potatoes and garlic in a covered pot in 2 in. lightly salted water 15 minutes or until fork tender. Drain; return to pot.

2 Add milk, butter, salt and pepper. Using handheld electric mixer or potato masher, beat or mash (some lumps may remain).

3 To serve: Stir in kale. Reheat, if needed.

Potato-Pear Gratin

6 large baking potatoes (about 3 1/2 lb), peeled
1 Tbsp salt
1 tsp pepper
1/2 tsp ground nutmeg
2 cans (15 oz each) pear halves in light syrup, drained,
* thinly sliced*
3/4 cup (3 oz) shredded Swiss cheese
1 cup heavy cream

1 Heat oven to 350°F. Grease a 13 x 9-in. or other shallow 3-qt baking dish.

2 Thinly slice potatoes, placing them in a large bowl of cold water. Drain in a colander and pat dry with paper towels. Dry bowl, add potatoes, sprinkle with salt, pepper and nutmeg and toss to coat.

3 Arrange 1/3 of the potatoes, slices overlapping, in prepared dish. Top with 1/3 of the pears, then 1/3 of the cheese. Repeat layers twice. Pour cream evenly over top.

4 Bake 1 hr 10 min or until potatoes are tender when pierced. Let stand 10 minutes before serving.

TIME: 1 hr 50 min

SERVES 12

PER SERVING: 218 cal,
  5 g pro, 27 g car, 2 g fiber,
  8 g fat (6 g saturated fat),
  34 mg chol, 617 mg sod

PLANNING TIP *The potatoes can be peeled and refrigerated in water to cover up to 1 day.*

TIME: 3 hr 45 min

SERVES 18

PER SERVING: 286 cal,
  33 g pro, 4 g car, 1 g fiber,
  14 g fat (5 g saturated fat),
  106 mg chol, 288 mg sod

PLANNING TIP *Can roast up to 2 days before serving.*

TIP *Ask your butcher to bone the turkey breast, leaving the skin on, and be sure to have cheesecloth, 5 poultry skewers and kitchen twine.*

LIME-CILANTRO SAUCE

1 cup light mayonnaise
3/4 cup plain lowfat yogurt
2 cups loosely packed cilantro
2 tsp minced garlic
1 tsp finely grated lime peel
1 Tbsp fresh lime juice

Purée all ingredients in blender or food processor. Refrigerate until ready to serve.

TIME: 15 min

MAKES 2 cups

PER 2 TBSP: 58 cal, 1 g pro,
  2 g car, 0 g fiber, 5 g fat
  (1 g saturated fat), 6 mg chol,
  123 mg sod

Stuffed Turkey Breast

One 6-lb whole turkey breast, boned; skin left on

STUFFING
  4 slices firm white bread, torn small
  3/4 cup heavy cream
  1 large egg
  1/2 tsp salt
  1/4 tsp each ground nutmeg and dried thyme
  2 Tbsp cognac (optional)
  1 cup finely chopped ham
  1/2 cup shelled pistachio nuts
  1/3 cup finely chopped red bell pepper

Lime-Cilantro Sauce (see recipe, left)

1 Place turkey breast skin side down on work surface and spread open. Cut off fat and discard. Trim enough meat from edges to make 1 1/2 cups small pieces, leaving at least a 1-in. border of skin extending beyond meat on all sides. Return turkey breast to refrigerator.

2 In food processor, process turkey pieces, bread, cream, egg, salt, nutmeg, thyme and cognac until a paste forms. Stir in the ham, pistachio nuts and red bell pepper.

3 Heat oven to 350°F. Have ready a shallow roasting pan with rack.

4 Cut cheesecloth 10 in. larger than the turkey breast. Spray cloth with nonstick cooking spray. Place turkey skin side down on middle. Spread with stuffing.

5 Using 4 to 5 poultry skewers, thread skin border and gather to enclose meat and stuffing in a ball. Pull up 4 corners of cloth and tie tightly.

6 Cut 4 long pieces kitchen twine. Place like spokes of a wheel, overlapping in center. Place turkey skin side down on top; tie up tightly.

7 Place skin side down on rack. Roast 1 hour. Turn right side up and roast 2 hours longer or until a meat thermometer inserted in center registers 165°F.

8 Cool, wrap in plastic wrap and refrigerate up to 2 days.

9 To SERVE: Cut twine, carefully peel off cheesecloth, then slice turkey breast. Serve with Lime-Cilantro Sauce.

Fruited White and Wild Rice Salad

1 1/2 cups uncooked converted white rice
1 1/3 cups (8 oz) uncooked wild rice
1 cup chopped celery
1 cup thinly sliced scallions
3/4 cup dried cranberries
3/4 cup snipped dried apricots

VINAIGRETTE DRESSING
  1/4 cup chicken broth
  1/4 cup red-wine vinegar
  1/4 cup olive oil
  2 tsp Dijon mustard
  1/2 tsp each salt and pepper

1 cup toasted pecans, chopped

1 Cook rices separately according to package directions. Drain wild rice well.

2 When cool, stir in the celery, scallions, and dried cranberries and apricots. Cover and refrigerate.

3 Shake Dressing ingredients in a covered jar until blended. Refrigerate.

4 To SERVE: Shake dressing to mix. Add with pecans to the rice mixture. Toss to mix and coat.

TIME: 1 hr

SERVES 12

PER SERVING: 301 cal, 6 g pro, 46 g car, 4 g fiber, 11 g fat (1 g saturated fat), 0 mg chol, 151 mg sod

PLANNING TIP: *Make vinaigrette and toast pecans up to 5 days ahead. Cook rice and add all ingredients except dressing and pecans up to 1 day ahead.*

TIME: 25 min

SERVES 12

PER SERVING: 178 cal,
  6 g pro, 14 g car, 4 g fiber,
  12 g fat (3 g saturated fat),
  7 mg chol, 405 mg sod

PLANNING TIP *The Dressing and salad greens may be prepared 1 day ahead. Refrigerate separately. Toast nuts up to 3 days ahead; store at room temperature.*

Christmas Salad

DRESSING
  1/3 cup olive oil
  3 Tbsp each balsamic vinegar and orange juice
  2 Tbsp Dijon mustard, preferably country style
  2 tsp sugar
  1/2 tsp pepper

18 cups torn mixed salad greens (such as red leaf, romaine, chicory)
2 cans (14 to 16 oz each) small to medium whole beets, drained well, cut in half
1/2 cup walnut pieces, toasted
4 oz blue cheese, crumbled

1 Shake Dressing ingredients in a covered jar to blend.

2 To SERVE: Place greens in serving bowl. Arrange beets, walnuts and cheese on top. Add Dressing; toss to mix and coat.

Lemon-Poached Pears with Two Sauces

2 Tbsp lemon juice
12 small, ripe, firm Bosc or Forelle pears with stems
3 cups water
1 cup sugar
3 slices lemon

RASPBERRY SAUCE
  2 bags (12 oz each) unsweetened frozen raspberries, thawed
  1 cup sugar

12 fresh mint sprigs

VANILLA SAUCE
  1 pt inexpensive vanilla ice cream, melted (see Tip)

1 Have ready a pot large enough to hold pears upright in a single layer.

2 Half-fill a large bowl with cold water. Stir in lemon juice. Peel pears, leaving stems on. Put pears in lemon water to prevent browning.

3 Bring water, sugar and lemon slices to boil in pot. Add pears, reduce heat, cover and simmer 20 to 25 minutes until tender when pierced at bottom.

4 Cool in pot, discard lemon slices and refrigerate pears in syrup until chilled.

5 RASPBERRY SAUCE: Stir raspberries through a strainer to make seedless purée. Stir in sugar. (Makes about 2 2/3 cups.)

6 TO SERVE: Pierce a hole in top of each pear and insert mint sprigs. Have ready 12 dessert plates. Spoon Raspberry Sauce on half of each plate, Vanilla Sauce on the other half. With a toothpick, starting in middle of each plate, draw a spiral through both sauces in increasingly larger circles to edge of plate. Set pear in center.

TIME: 50 min

SERVES 12

PER SERVING: 288 cal, 2 g pro, 68 g car, 4 g fiber, 4 g fat (2 g saturated fat), 10 mg chol, 19 mg sod

PLANNING TIP Poach pears up to 1 day before serving them. Refrigerate, covered, in syrup. Make the Raspberry Sauce up to 2 days ahead and refrigerate.

TIP Use inexpensive vanilla ice cream for the Vanilla Sauce, since it tends to be thicker when melted than premium brands.

TIME: About 1 hr, plus 1 hr 30 min chilling

SERVES 12

PER SERVING: 459 cal, 7 g pro, 65 g car, 2 g fiber, 20 g fat (11 g saturated fat), 165 mg chol, 148 mg sod

PLANNING TIP *The custard and the sauce can be made up to 3 days ahead. Refrigerate in airtight containers. The trifle can be prepared up to 12 hours ahead.*

TIP *If you're pressed for time or want a layered look, there's no need to make the decorations around the inside of bowl. Instead, cut and layer the cake with the cranberry sauce and plain custard, ending with the chocolate custard.*

Cranberry-Chocolate Trifle

CUSTARD
 3/4 cup sugar
 1/3 cup cornstarch
 4 cups 1% lowfat milk
 Yolks from 6 large eggs
 1 cup semisweet chocolate chips
 1 cup heavy (whipping) cream

CRANBERRY SAUCE
 1 bag (12 oz) cranberries (3 cups)
 1 cup sugar
 1/2 cup orange juice

One 10 3/4-oz frozen poundcake, thawed
1 Tbsp sugar
1 Tbsp Grand Marnier
GARNISH: chocolate shaved off a bar with a vegetable peeler

1 Have ready a 2 1/2-qt glass serving bowl, preferably straight-sided.

2 CUSTARD: Whisk sugar and cornstarch in medium saucepan to mix. Whisk in milk, then egg yolks, taking care to get into corners of pan. Cook over medium heat, stirring occasionally, until boiling and thickened, about 10 minutes. Reduce heat to medium-low and cook 2 minutes longer (to eliminate cornstarch taste). Pour 3/4 cup into small bowl. Stir in chocolate chips until melted, then 1/2 cup heavy cream. Pour remaining custard into another bowl. Place plastic wrap directly on surface of both. Refrigerate until cold.

3 MEANWHILE MAKE CRANBERRY SAUCE: Bring all ingredients to boil in medium saucepan. Cook, stirring occasionally, 10 minutes until cranberries pop and sauce thickens. Pour into bowl. Cover and refrigerate until cold.

4 TO MAKE DECORATIONS FOR SIDE OF BOWL: Cut 1/2

in. off top of cake; reserve. Cut cake crosswise in nine 1/4-in.-thick slices and five 1/2-in.-thick slices (as if slicing bread). Working with a few at a time, place 1/4-in.-thick slices between sheets of wax paper. With rolling pin, roll slices very thin. Remove top sheet and spread 1 tsp Cranberry Sauce over each slice. One by one, loosen slices from bottom sheet with a long metal spatula, then, starting at narrow end, roll up jelly-roll fashion. With very sharp knife (to cut cranberries), cut each crosswise into 4 equal rounds; set aside. Spread 1 Tbsp cranberry sauce over each 1/2-in. cake slice, then cut each corner to corner, forming 2 triangles.

5 TO ASSEMBLE: Cut reserved cake top and remaining poundcake in cubes. Press plain side of cake triangles against sides of serving bowl, placing half the cubes in bottom of bowl to hold triangles in place. Firmly press rounds against bowl, resting on triangles as shown (right). Top cubes with half the remaining cranberry sauce. Carefully, a spoonful at a time, spoon half the plain custard on top. Repeat layers with remaining cake cubes, cranberry sauce and plain custard. Spoon chocolate custard over top and cover with plastic wrap. Refrigerate up to 12 hours.

6 UP TO 30 MINUTES BEFORE SERVING: Beat remaining 1/2 cup heavy cream, the sugar and Grand Marnier in a medium bowl on high speed until stiff peaks form when beaters are lifted. Drop spoonfuls on trifle; garnish with chocolate shavings.

TIME: 1 hr
DECORATE: About 15 min

SERVES 10

PER SERVING (without
decorations): 517 cal, 7 g pro,
75 g car, 2 g fiber, 24 g fat
(14 g saturated fat),
130 mg chol, 185 mg sod

PLANNING TIP *Filling and frosting can be made 3 days ahead. Refrigerate. Cake can be prepared through Step 5 a day ahead. Wrap and refrigerate. Decorations can be made 1 week ahead. Wrap; refrigerate separately. To assemble, bring cake and frosting to room temperature. Beat frosting until spreadable.*

TIP *Chocolate twigs can be found in specialty food shops and some supermarkets. Look for them in the candy/chocolate aisle.*

Yule Log

FILLING

2 cups half-and-half

1 box (5.1 oz) instant vanilla pudding and pie filling
(6-serving size)

3/4 tsp instant espresso powder

1/4 tsp ground cinnamon

CAKE

4 large eggs, at room temperature

2/3 cup sugar

1 tsp vanilla extract

2/3 cup flour

3 Tbsp unsweetened cocoa powder

FROSTING

1 stick (1/2 cup) butter, softened

4 oz unsweetened baking chocolate, melted according to
package directions

1 lb confectioners' sugar

About 3 Tbsp milk

1/2 tsp vanilla extract

DECORATIONS: Chocolate Leaves, Marshmallow Mushrooms,
Pinecones (see directions, opposite page), chocolate twigs
(see Tip)

1 FILLING: Beat all ingredients as directed for pudding. Refrigerate 1 hour or until set.

2 Meanwhile heat oven to 350°F. Grease bottom and sides of a 15 1/2 x 10 1/2-in. rimmed baking sheet. Line with wax paper, then grease the paper.

3 CAKE: Beat eggs, sugar and vanilla in a large bowl on high speed 8 minutes until very thick and tripled in volume. Sprinkle with flour; fold in with a rubber spatula just until blended. Spread in prepared pan.

4 Bake 13 to 15 minutes or until golden around edges.

Cool in pan on wire rack 5 minutes or until pan can be handled without potholders. Meanwhile lay a kitchen towel (not terry) on countertop. Stirring cocoa through a strainer, dust towel area the size of the cake evenly with cocoa.

5 Invert cake on towel. Lift off pan and carefully peel off paper. Roll up cake and towel from a long side. Cool on rack.

6 UP TO 3 HOURS BEFORE SERVING: Unroll cake. Spread filling to within 1 in. of all edges. Reroll, from same end as before. Transfer to serving platter. Refrigerate.

7 FROSTING: Beat butter and chocolate in large bowl until blended. Add confectioners' sugar, 3 Tbsp milk and vanilla and beat to mix, adding more milk if needed, 1 tsp at a time, until spreading consistency.

8 TO ASSEMBLE: Cut a 2 1/2-in. diagonal slice off one end of cake. Use frosting to glue end (stump) to cake. Leave ends of log and stump unfrosted. Frost cake to resemble bark. Decorate as shown.

CHOCOLATE LEAVES

Wash rose or lemon leaves, rinse and pat dry. Brush undersides with melted milk or semisweet chocolate. Refrigerate on wax paper–lined pan until hard. Carefully, but quickly, so chocolate doesn't melt, peel off green leaf.

MARSHMALLOW MUSHROOMS

For caps, flatten 6 large marshmallows with a rolling pin. Shape caps over top of a finger. Cut 3 marshmallows in half lengthwise; roll each between palms to make stems. Moisten 1 end with water and press onto cap. Dip top of caps in cocoa powder; brush off excess.

PINECONES

Place 4 Tbsp-size mounds of frosting 3 in. apart on a large wax paper–lined plate. Cut 2 large marshmallows in half lengthwise. Press 1 half, cut side down, onto each mound. Generously spread frosting over top and sides. Insert sliced almonds (with skin) into frosting to simulate pinecones. Refrigerate until frosting hardens.

Christmas Menu for 12

CHRISTMAS ANTIPASTO

SAVORY SALMON AND DILL DANISH

CHEESE SNOWFLAKES

SHRIMP ON TOAST STARS

FRUIT SALAD WITH CRANBERRY DRESSING

SAVORY BREAD PUDDING

PORK ROAST WITH FRUIT COMPOTE

WHIPPED SWEET POTATOES

BEANS & PEAS WITH PECANS

CHOCOLATE-HAZELNUT TORTE

RASPBERRY SWIRL CHEESECAKE

CREAM PUFF CHRISTMAS TREES

CLOCKWISE FROM TOP LEFT: Whipped Sweet Potatoes, Fruit Compote, Pork Roast

TIME: 20 min

SERVES 12

PER SERVING: 181 cal, 7 g pro,
   13 g car, 4 g fiber, 12 g fat
   (4 g saturated fat), 19 mg
   chol, 633 mg sod

PLANNING TIP *Prepare in the morning, cover and refrigerate.*

TIP *Other marinated vegetables or cheeses may be substituted.*

NOTE *This blend of peppercorns can be found in your market's spice section. One commonly found brand calls it Peppercorn Melange. To crush, place peppercorns in a sturdy plastic food bag and hit with bottom of a heavy skillet.*

Christmas Antipasto

One 12-oz jar each marinated roasted peppers (red and yellow), preferably in olive oil; marinated chickpeas; and quartered marinated artichoke hearts
1 tub (9 oz) cherry-size fresh mozzarella cheese balls
1 jar (7 oz) mixed country olives
2 Tbsp golden or dark raisins
1 Tbsp pine nuts or slivered almonds
2 tsp finely chopped parsley
1 tsp peppercorns, preferably a blend of black, green, pink and white pepper, coarsely crushed (see Note)
6 lettuce leaves

1 Drain peppers, chickpeas, artichokes, cheese balls and olives. In medium bowl, mix peppers with raisins and pine nuts. In a small bowl, mix cheese balls with parsley and peppercorns.

2 TO SERVE: Arrange the vegetables and cheese on a lettuce-lined platter.

Savory Salmon and Dill Danish

FILLING

  1 brick (8 oz) 1/3-less-fat cream cheese (Neufchâtel), softened
  1 large egg
  4 oz smoked salmon, coarsely chopped
  1/4 cup grated Parmesan cheese
  1/4 cup chopped fresh dill
  3 Tbsp thinly sliced scallions
  1 1/2 tsp freshly grated lemon peel

1 sheet frozen puff pastry (from a 17 1/2-oz box), thawed as
  directed on box

1 large egg beaten with 1 tsp water

GARNISH: quartered lemon slices and dill sprigs

1 FILLING: Beat cream cheese in a medium bowl with mixer on high speed until smooth. On low speed, beat in egg just until blended. Stir in remaining ingredients. Refrigerate while preparing pastry.

2 Heat oven to 425°F. Have a baking sheet ready.

3 Unroll pastry on a lightly floured surface. With a lightly floured rolling pin, roll to a 12 x 9-in. rectangle. With a sharp knife or pastry wheel, cut three 1-in.-wide strips from 1 long side.

4 Transfer pastry rectangle to the baking sheet. Brush a narrow border of egg on all sides. Lightly press 1 pastry strip on each long side to form border. Cut third strip in half crosswise; press a half on each short side. Brush strips with egg. Spread filling in border.

5 Bake 12 minutes, reduce heat to 375°F and bake 10 to 12 minutes more until puffed and pastry is golden brown. Remove to a wire rack to cool.

6 TO SERVE: Cut in thirds lengthwise, then in sixths crosswise. Garnish with lemon and dill. Serve at room temperature.

TIME: About 55 minutes

MAKES 18 pieces

PER PIECE: 128 cal, 5 g pro,
  6 g car, 0 g fiber, 9 g fat
  (3 g saturated fat), 35 mg chol,
  242 mg sod

PLANNING TIP *Bake up to 1 day ahead. Refrigerate loosely covered. Bring to room temperature before serving.*

TIME: 46 min (includes
         baking 2 batches)

MAKES 24

PER 2 SNOWFLAKES: 76 cal,
 6 g pro, 0 g car, 0 g fiber,
 5 g fat (4 g saturated fat),
 17 mg chol, 120 mg sod

PLANNING TIP *Bake snowflakes up to 3 days ahead. Store in a covered rigid container at room temperature.*

TIP *These crisps are fragile. Handle them carefully.*

COOKING LESSON

Spread the shredded cheese into 3 1/2-in. rounds with uneven edges.

Cheese Snowflakes

8-oz wedge Parmesan cheese, preferably good quality such as Parmigiano-Reggiano, rind removed

1 Heat oven to 375°F. Line baking sheet(s) with foil. Coat with nonstick cooking spray.

2 Shred the cheese using large holes of a box grater or shredding disk of a food processor.

3 Drop shredded cheese by slightly rounded tablespoonfuls 3 in. apart onto the foil-lined baking sheet(s). Spread each into a 3 1/2-in. round (see Cooking Lesson, left).

4 Bake 6 to 8 minutes until pale golden. Let cool, then gently peel each off foil.

Shrimp on Toast Stars

CILANTRO MAYONNAISE
1 cup lightly packed cilantro
1/2 cup light mayonnaise
2 tsp lemon juice

2 tsp olive oil
36 (about 1 1/4 lb) medium-to-large shrimp, peeled, deveined (see Cooking Lesson, below) and patted dry
2 tsp fajita seasoning
1/4 tsp salt
About 18 slices firm white and/or pumpernickel bread
GARNISH: cilantro leaves

1 Have ready a metal 3-in. star and/or a 2-in. round cookie cutter.

2 CILANTRO MAYONNAISE: Process ingredients in a food processor until smooth.

3 Heat oil in large nonstick skillet over medium heat. Add shrimp and cook, turning shrimp a few times, 2 minutes until almost cooked through. Stir in seasoning and salt and cook 1 minute longer or until cooked through. Let cool.

4 Toast bread. When cool, use cookie cutter to cut out 36 stars or rounds.

5 To SERVE: Place toasts on serving plates. Top each with a dollop of Cilantro Mayonnaise and a shrimp. Garnish with cilantro.

COOKING LESSON

Use a shrimp peeler to peel and devein the shrimp in one easy step. Available, often for less than $1, in stores and supermarkets selling kitchenware.

TIME: 40 min

SERVES 12

PER SERVING: 158 cal, 10 g pro, 15 g car, 1 g fiber, 6 g fat (1 g saturated fat), 62 mg chol, 367 mg sod

PLANNING TIP *The Cilantro Mayonnaise can be made up to 2 days ahead. The shrimp can be cooked and the toasts cut out up to 1 day ahead. Refrigerate the mayonnaise and shrimp separately; store toasts at room temperature. Assemble just before serving.*

TIME: 25 min

SERVES 12

PER SERVING: 116 cal, 1 g pro,
25 g car, 2 g fiber, 2 g fat
(0 g saturated fat), 0 mg chol,
153 mg sod

PLANNING TIP *The dressing can be made up to 3 days ahead. Refrigerate covered. Step 2 can be completed up to 2 hours before serving. Refrigerate covered.*

TIP *Other bagged lettuce blends or 1 lb mesclun (mixed baby salad greens) may be substituted.*

Fruit Salad with Cranberry Dressing

CRANBERRY DRESSING
3/4 cup bottled red-wine vinaigrette
1/3 cup frozen cranberry-juice cocktail concentrate
1/2 cup dried cranberries
1 1/2 Tbsp honey, or to taste

2 each apples and ripe pears, quartered, cored, sliced in wedges
2 cups seedless grapes, cut in halves
2 bags (10 oz each) European Blend Salad (see Tip)

1 CRANBERRY DRESSING: Whisk ingredients in small bowl.

2 Put fruits in a large bowl (not the serving bowl). Add half the dressing and toss to mix and coat. Put remaining dressing in a cruet or small pitcher.

3 TO SERVE: Place greens in serving bowl. Top with fruits and dressing from bottom of fruit bowl. Spoon fruits and lettuce on salad plates; pass dressing in cruet at the table.

Savory Bread Pudding

2 Tbsp stick butter
1 cup finely chopped onion
1 lb sliced assorted mushrooms (see Tip) or 2 pkg
 (8 to 10 oz each) sliced white mushrooms
1/4 tsp each salt and pepper
1/4 cup finely chopped parsley
1 loaf (8 oz) French bread, cut in 1/2-in.-thick slices
6 large eggs
3 cups whole milk
1 tub (6.5 oz) light garlic-and-herb spreadable cheese
 (such as Alouette)
1/2 cup freshly grated Parmesan cheese

1 Heat oven to 325°F. Grease a shallow 2 1/2-qt baking dish.

2 Melt 1 Tbsp butter in large nonstick skillet. Add 1/2 the onion and 1/2 the mushrooms; sauté over medium-high heat 4 minutes or until tender and browned. Place in a medium bowl. Repeat with remaining butter, onion and mushrooms. Stir in salt, pepper and parsley.

3 Scatter 1/2 the mushroom mixture in prepared dish. Top with bread, slices slightly overlapping. Scatter remaining mushrooms over top. In a large bowl, whisk eggs, milk and spreadable cheese until blended (small bits of cheese may remain). Pour evenly over bread. Sprinkle with Parmesan cheese.

4 Bake 1 hour or until puffed and golden brown, and a knife inserted near center comes out clean.

TIME: 1 hr 30 min

SERVES 12

PER SERVING: 215 cal, 11 g pro, 17 g car, 1 g fiber, 12 g fat (6 g saturated fat), 134 mg chol, 379 mg sod

PLANNING TIP *Prepare pudding through Step 3 up to 1 day ahead. Refrigerate covered. Bake in oven along with pork, using other oven rack.*

TIP *Including some exotic mushrooms, such as shiitake and crimini, gives this dish a delightful woodsy flavor. If using shiitake, discard the tough stems.*

TIME: About 2 hr to
         2 hr 50 min

SERVES 12 (with leftovers)

PER SERVING (4 oz pork with
 1/4 cup compote): 356 cal,
 34 g pro, 20 g car, 2 g fiber,
 14 g fat (6 g saturated fat),
 100 mg chol, 466 mg sod

PLANNING TIP *The compote can be made up to 1 week ahead. Refrigerate covered.*

TIP *While the cooked roast rests, the internal temperature will continue to rise to the desired degree of doneness.*

Pork Roast with Fruit Compote

FRUIT COMPOTE
 1 large lemon
 3 Tbsp stick butter
 1 cup chopped onion
 1 cup dry white wine or apple cider
 18 dried Calimyrna figs (about 8 oz), cut in 4 wedges
 12 dried apricot halves (about 3 oz), coarsely chopped
 2 Tbsp honey

5-lb boneless center-cut pork loin roast, tied
1 1/2 Tbsp dried sage
1 1/2 tsp salt
3/4 tsp pepper
1 cup chicken broth
GARNISH: *lemon wedges, sugar-coated cranberries and fresh sage leaves*

1 Heat oven to 325°F. Have ready a shallow roasting pan fitted with a rack.

2 FRUIT COMPOTE: With a vegetable peeler, peel yellow part of peel (zest) from lemon in strips. Squeeze juice (1/4 cup). Melt butter in a medium saucepan. Add onion and sauté until translucent. Add lemon peel, juice and remaining ingredients. Bring to a boil; reduce heat, cover and simmer gently, stirring occasionally, 15 minutes or until fruits are soft.

3 Meanwhile rub roast with sage, salt and pepper, and place on rack in pan.

4 Bake, for medium doneness, 1 hour 40 minutes or until a meat thermometer inserted in center reads 150°F (see Tip). For well-done, bake 2 1/2 hours until 160°F. Place on a large serving platter; cover loosely with foil and let rest 15 minutes (temperature will rise to 155° for medium, 165° for well-done).

5 Meanwhile discard fat from roasting pan. Place pan on 2 burners over medium heat. Add chicken broth and

cook, scraping up browned bits on bottom of pan.

6 Add compote and simmer 5 to 10 minutes to thicken slightly. Remove lemon peel; pour compote (you'll have 3 cups) into a serving dish or gravy boat. Garnish platter; serve compote with pork.

Whipped Sweet Potatoes

5 lb sweet potatoes, scrubbed and pierced with a fork
3/4 cup apple cider or juice
3 Tbsp maple syrup
1 Tbsp lemon juice
1/2 tsp each salt and pepper

1 Heat oven to 400°F. Place potatoes on a rimmed baking sheet.

2 Bake 1 hr or until very soft. Let stand until cool enough to handle.

3 Cut each potato in half and scrape pulp into a large bowl. Add remaining ingredients and mash with a potato masher or beat with mixer until blended and smooth.

Beans & Peas with Pecans

1 1/2 lb fresh green beans, stem ends trimmed, beans cut crosswise in thirds (3 1/4 cups)
1 bag (20 oz) frozen green peas
3 Tbsp stick butter
1/2 tsp each salt and pepper
3/4 cup toasted chopped pecans (see Toasting Nuts, page 28)

1 Steam beans or cook in a pot of boiling water 7 to 8 minutes until tender. Drain.

2 Cook peas as directed on pkg. Drain.

3 Melt the butter in a pot over medium heat. Stir in beans, peas, salt and pepper. Cook, tossing to heat through. Stir in the toasted pecans.

TIME: 1 hr 20 min

SERVES 12

PER SERVING: 163 cal, 2 g pro, 38 g car, 4 g fiber, 0 g fat (0 g saturated fat), 0 mg chol, 115 mg sod

TIME: 20 min

SERVES 12

PER SERVING: 123 cal, 4 g pro, 11 g car, 3 g fiber, 8 g fat (2 g saturated fat), 8 mg chol, 182 mg sod

PLANNING TIP *Toast nuts up to 1 week ahead and store airtight at room temperature. Cook peas and beans up to 2 days ahead. Refrigerate covered.*

TIME: 2 hr 10 min

SERVES 16

PER SERVING: 366 cal, 5 g pro, 29 g car, 1 g fiber, 27 g fat (10 g saturated fat), 51 mg chol, 50 mg sod

PLANNING TIP *Assemble and frost the torte at least 8 hours or up to 2 days before serving. Meringue layers will gradually soften; that's OK.*

COOKING LESSON

For each baked layer, spread a third of the meringue-hazelnut mixture evenly within the lines traced on the floured, greased baking sheets.

Chocolate-Hazelnut Torte

MERINGUE LAYERS

- 1 3/4 cups (about 7 oz) hazelnuts, toasted (see Note 1, opposite page)
- 1 cup plus 3 Tbsp sugar
- Whites from 6 large eggs
- 1 Tbsp vanilla extract
- 1/4 tsp cider vinegar

FILLING

- 1 cup heavy (whipping) cream
- 1 cup (from a 13-oz jar) chocolate-hazelnut spread (such as Nutella; see Note 2, opposite page)

FROSTING

- 1 1/2 cups heavy (whipping) cream
- 1 Tbsp sugar
- 1 tsp vanilla extract

DECORATION: *skinned, toasted hazelnuts; purchased chocolate leaves and chocolate twigs; red ribbon*

1 Position racks to divide oven in thirds. Heat to 250°F. Lightly grease and flour 2 large baking sheets. Cut wax paper into a 12 x 4-in. rectangle. Using paper as a pattern and the tip of a pointed knife, trace outline of 2 rectangles 2 in. apart in flour on 1 baking sheet and 1 rectangle on the other.

2 In food processor (or 2 batches in blender), process 1 1/2 cups hazelnuts (save rest for decoration) and 1 cup sugar until powdery.

3 Beat egg whites in a large bowl with mixer on low speed until foamy. Beat in vanilla and vinegar. Increase speed to high and beat until stiff peaks form when beaters are lifted. Sprinkle with remaining 3 Tbsp sugar and beat 1 minute longer.

4 Sprinkle nut mixture on egg whites. Fold in gently with a rubber spatula until well blended. (Whites will deflate somewhat; that's OK.) Divide in thirds and spread

evenly within traced rectangles on baking sheets (see Cooking Lesson, opposite page).

5 Bake 1 baking sheet on each oven rack, switching position of sheets halfway through baking, 1 hour 40 minutes or until meringues are dry and can be easily loosened. Carefully (meringues break easily; see Tip) lift layers by running a long spatula under each. Place on a wire rack and let cool completely.

6 MEANWHILE MAKE FILLING: Beat cream in a medium bowl with mixer on medium speed until soft peaks form when beaters are lifted. Put chocolate-hazelnut spread in another medium bowl. Stir in 1/2 cup whipped cream, then fold in remaining cream until blended and a mousse-like texture. Refrigerate to firm up while meringue layers bake and cool.

7 TO ASSEMBLE: Place 1 meringue layer on a serving platter. Spread with half the Filling. Repeat with another meringue and remaining filling. Top with remaining meringue. Press down evenly and gently.

8 FROSTING: Beat ingredients in a large bowl with mixer on medium speed until soft peaks form when beaters are lifted. Spread over sides, then top of cake. Refrigerate until ready to serve.

9 TO SERVE: Decorate the torte with hazelnuts, chocolate leaves and chocolate twigs tied with ribbon. Cut with a serrated knife.

NOTE 1 *To toast nuts, spread in a baking pan and bake at 350°F 12 to 15 minutes until fragrant and the papery skins start to flake. Cool slightly, then rub between hands to remove most of the skins.*

NOTE 2 *Look for chocolate-hazelnut spread in the peanut butter section of your market.*

TIP *If the meringue layers break while being removed from the baking sheets, they can be glued together with the filling.*

Time: 1 hr 23 min, plus 12 hr chilling

Serves 12

Per serving (with 2 1/2 Tbsp sauce): 297 cal, 5 g pro, 51 g car, 0 g fiber, 9 g fat (4 g saturated fat), 55 mg chol, 132 mg sod

Raspberry Swirl Cheesecake

1/2 cup graham cracker crumbs (about 4 whole crackers; see Tip, opposite page)

2 bags (12 oz each) thawed frozen, unsweetened raspberries

2 cups sugar

1/4 cup cornstarch

1/4 cup raspberry cordial (such as Chambord) or cran-raspberry juice cocktail

2 Tbsp fresh lemon juice

4 bricks (8 oz each) 1/3-less-fat cream cheese (Neufchâtel), softened

2 large eggs

1 cup reduced-fat sour cream

2 tsp vanilla extract

DECORATION: fresh mint sprigs

1 Heat oven to 325°F. Lightly grease an 8-in. springform pan. Sprinkle cracker crumbs over bottom.

2 Stir and press raspberries with back of a spoon through a strainer set over a medium saucepan. Discard seeds and pulp. Whisk in 1 cup sugar and 2 Tbsp cornstarch. Bring to a gentle boil and cook, whisking constantly, 1 to 2 minutes until thick. Remove from heat; stir in cordial and lemon juice. Let cool to room temperature while preparing cheesecake.

3 Mix remaining 1 cup sugar and 2 Tbsp cornstarch in a large bowl. Add cream cheese and beat with mixer on medium speed until smooth. Reduce speed to low and beat in eggs just until blended. Beat in sour cream and vanilla.

4 Pour half into the prepared pan. Spoon on 1/3 cup raspberry sauce in 2 concentric circles. Add remaining batter and spoon on 1/3 cup more sauce as before. (Refrigerate remaining 2 cups sauce.) Using a table knife, cut through batter in figure-eights for a marbleized effect, being careful not to disturb crumb crust.

5 Bake 1 hour 10 minutes or until a pick inserted near center of cake comes out clean, but center is still jiggly. Run a thin knife between edges of cake and pan. Cool in pan on a wire rack (jiggly portion will set completely as cake cools). Cover loosely and refrigerate at least 12 hours or up to 3 days.

6 To SERVE: Remove pan sides. Cut in wedges, drizzle with reserved raspberry sauce and garnish with mint.

PLANNING TIP *Bake the cake at least 12 hours or up to 3 days before serving.*

TIP *Crush graham crackers into crumbs in a food processor. Or put in sturdy ziptop plastic bag and crush with a rolling pin.*

TIME: About 1 hr, plus 30
        min for freezing

SERVES 12

PER SERVING: 485 cal, 8 g pro,
72 g car, 0 g fiber, 19 g fat
(10 g saturated fat), 156 mg
chol, 217 mg sod

PLANNING TIP *The filled cream puffs may be frozen up to 1 week. Prepare through Step 6. Transfer frozen puffs to an air-tight container and freeze.*

TIP *Crush candy canes in a food processor, or put them in a sturdy plastic food bag and tap firmly with a heavy skillet.*

Cream Puff Christmas Trees

CREAM PUFFS
1 stick (1/2 cup) butter
1 1/2 cups water
1 1/2 cups flour
6 large eggs, at room temperature

3 pt peppermint-stick ice cream
1 1/2 cups bottled good-quality hot fudge sauce
4 peppermint candy canes, finely crushed (see Tip)

1 Position racks to divide oven in thirds. Heat to 400°F. Lightly grease 2 large baking sheets.

2 Bring butter and water to boil in a heavy 3-qt saucepan until butter melts. Over low heat, add flour all at once. Stir vigorously with a wooden spoon until mixture forms ball and leaves sides of pan. Remove from heat; let stand 2 minutes.

3 With mixer on medium speed, beat in eggs, 1 at a time, until dough is smooth and no longer looks slippery.

4 Drop rounded teaspoonfuls dough 3/4 in. apart onto prepared baking sheets. (You'll need 108 for 12 servings. This recipe lets you make a few extra.)

5 Bake 1 baking sheet on each oven rack, switching position of sheets halfway through baking, 20 to 25 minutes until puffs are puffed, golden and firm. Remove to a wire rack to cool completely.

6 Chill a baking sheet in freezer about 10 minutes. Meanwhile cut puffs in half horizontally. Working quickly, fill bottoms with ice cream, then replace tops. Place on the chilled sheet, cover with plastic wrap and freeze until firm.

7 TO SERVE: Heat fudge sauce as directed on jar. On each dessert dish, arrange 5 cream puffs in a tight circle, topped by 3 and then 1 puff. Drizzle with fudge sauce and sprinkle with crushed candy canes.

Easter Lunch Menu for 12

Shrimp Salad Baskets

Spring Salad with Lemon-Chive Dressing

Spiral-Cut Ham

Egg & Asparagus Roll-Ups

Little Carrot Muffins

Lemon Cream Tart

Chocolate Nests

Easter Cake

Big Easter Egg Cookies

Spiral-Cut Ham

TIME: About 22 min

MAKES 24

PER 2 BASKETS: 106 cal,
  10 g pro, 6 g car, 0 g fiber,
  4 g fat (1 g saturated fat),
  72 mg chol, 212 mg sod

PLANNING TIP *The salad can
be made up to 1 day ahead
(bag the chopped radishes and
shrimp for garnish separately).
Refrigerate salad tightly covered.*

Shrimp Salad Baskets

1 1/2 lb (about 32 per lb) raw medium shrimp, peeled
  and deveined
1/3 cup light mayonnaise
2 Tbsp finely chopped fresh dill
1 1/2 Tbsp minced scallion
2 tsp fresh lemon juice
1/4 tsp salt
1/8 tsp hot-pepper sauce
1/2 cup finely chopped radishes
24 frozen mini fillo-pastry shells (from two 2.1-oz boxes), thawed
GARNISH: reserved shrimp (see Step 2) and fresh dill

1 Put shrimp with water to cover in a 2-qt saucepan.
Bring to a boil, reduce to a simmer, cover and cook 1 to 2
minutes until shrimp are cooked through. Drain in a colander, cool under running cold water, drain, then pat dry.

2 Reserve 24 shrimp for garnish. Finely chop rest and
place in a medium bowl; stir in remaining ingredients
except radishes and pastry shells.

3 NO MORE THAN 45 MINUTES BEFORE SERVING: Stir
radishes into salad. Fill shells, add garnish and refrigerate.

Spring Salad with Lemon-Chive Dressing

LEMON-CHIVE DRESSING

1 Tbsp freshly grated lemon peel

2 Tbsp fresh lemon juice

1 1/2 Tbsp Dijon mustard

1 1/2 Tbsp sherry-wine vinegar or red-wine vinegar

1/2 tsp each sugar, salt and freshly ground pepper

1/2 cup olive oil, preferably extra-virgin

2/3 cup finely chopped chives

12 oz fresh sugar snap peas, strings removed (see Tip)

1 lb yellow summer squash

4 to 5 medium carrots (about 10 oz), peeled

2 bags (5 to 6 oz each) mixed baby lettuce

1 pt grape tomatoes

1 DRESSING: Whisk lemon peel, juice, mustard, vinegar, sugar, salt and pepper in a medium bowl to blend. Gradually whisk in oil until thickened and blended.

2 Bring a medium pot of water to a boil. Add snap peas; boil 30 to 60 seconds until bright green and crisp-tender. Immediately drain in a colander, cool under cold running water and let drain.

3 With a vegetable peeler, pare thin strips down length of squash making ribbons no wider than 1/2 in. (discard seedy middle of squash). Pare carrots in strips the same way. Mix strips (you'll have about 8 cups).

4 On 12 salad plates, arrange baby lettuce. Top each serving with a mound of about 3/4 cup squash-carrot mixture. Make a depression in centers to form nests. Put 4 or 5 grape tomato "eggs" in middle of each; scatter snap peas around nests. Cover and refrigerate until serving.

5 JUST BEFORE SERVING: Add chives to dressing; spoon over salad.

TIME: About 40 min

SERVES 12

PER SERVING: 121 cal, 2 g pro, 8 g car, 2 g fiber, 10 g fat (1 g saturated fat), 0 mg chol, 154 mg sod

PLANNING TIP *Up to 2 days ahead, make Dressing through Step 1 and refrigerate in a covered jar; cut and wrap chives; and prepare and bag snap peas. Up to 1 day ahead, prepare carrots and squash. Bag and refrigerate. Prepare through Step 4 up to 4 hours before serving.*

TIP *To remove string from pea pod, grasp stem end and pull, removing string along the pod's straight side.*

Spiral-Cut Ham

Buy a spiral-cut precooked ham that can be served as is or heated. (Most now come either preglazed or with a glaze packet.) Smoked and cured presliced hams come complete with baking and serving directions.

HOW MUCH TO BUY: A 7- to 8-lb bone-in half ham (shank or butt) will feed 12 people with ample leftovers for sandwiches. And don't forget to save the bone to make split-pea or bean soup.

Egg & Asparagus Roll-Ups

3 lbs asparagus, each spear about 1/2 in. thick (you'll need 3 to 4 per roll-up)
12 oven-ready no-boil lasagna noodles (from an 8- or 9-oz box)
1 jar (16 oz) light Parmesan Alfredo sauce
1 1/3 cups 1% lowfat milk
1 tsp nutmeg, preferably freshly grated
8 oz Gruyère or Monterey Jack cheese, shredded (2 cups)
8 hard-cooked large eggs (reserve 2 for garnish)
GARNISH: sieved reserved hard-cooked eggs and 1/4 cup chopped parsley (see Note, opposite page)

1 Bring a large pot of water to boil. Have two 13 x 9-in. baking dishes ready.

2 Cut bottoms off asparagus to make 6-in.-long spears. Add to pot; boil 2 minutes or until crisp-tender. Remove with tongs to a colander; cool under gently running cold water. Drain well; pat dry.

3 Remove pot of boiling water from heat. Add noodles; let soak 5 to 6 minutes. Remove with a slotted pancake turner; spread out on paper towels to drain.

4 Meanwhile whisk Alfredo sauce, milk and nutmeg to blend. Spread 1/2 cup over bottom of each baking dish to cover.

TIME: About 1 hr 10 min

SERVES 12

PER ROLL-UP: 337 cal, 19 g pro, 28 g car, 2 g fiber, 17 g fat (9 g saturated fat), 185 mg chol, 469 mg sod

PLANNING TIP *Cook and peel eggs and shred cheese up to 3 days before using. Bag separately and refrigerate. Prepare roll-ups through Step 6 and the garnish up to 1 day ahead. Refrigerate.*

TIP *About 30 to 40 minutes before serving, remove ham from oven and tent loosely with foil. To bake roll-ups, position racks to divide oven in thirds and heat to 375°F.*

NOTE *Cut up reserved cooked eggs. Press with back of a wooden spoon through a strainer into a small bowl. Stir in parsley.*

5 FOR EACH ROLL-UP: Place 3 or 4 asparagus crosswise on a noodle. Sprinkle with 1 Tbsp cheese. With an egg slicer, cut 1 egg. Lay half the slices on the asparagus (save other half for another roll-up). Drizzle egg with 1 Tbsp Alfredo sauce; sprinkle with 1 Tbsp cheese. Roll noodle around filling; place seam side down in baking dish (you'll want 2 rows, 3 rolls per row, in each dish).

6 Continue making roll-ups, 6 per dish. Cover noodles completely with remaining Alfredo sauce; sprinkle with remaining cheese. Cover tightly with foil.

7 TO SERVE: Heat oven to 375°F. Bake, covered, 25 to 30 minutes until asparagus and noodles are tender and roll-ups are hot. Garnish with egg-parsley mixture.

TIME: About 1 hr 30 min
(includes baking
2 batches)

MAKES 24

PER 2 MUFFINS: 202 cal,
3 g pro, 36 g car, 1 g fiber,
5 g fat (1 g saturated fat),
18 mg chol, 233 mg sod

TIP *Grate the orange peel for the icing and wrap airtight, then juice the oranges for the muffins.*

Little Carrot Muffins

1 3/4 cups all-purpose flour
1/2 cup granulated sugar
1 3/4 tsp baking powder
1 1/2 tsp ground cinnamon
1/2 tsp nutmeg, preferably freshly grated
1/2 tsp each baking soda and salt
2 jars (4 oz each) baby food carrots
3/4 cup freshly squeezed orange juice (see Tip)
1/4 cup vegetable oil
1 large egg
1 tsp vanilla extract

ORANGE ICING
 1 cup confectioners' sugar
 1 Tbsp 1% lowfat milk
 1 tsp freshly grated orange peel
 1/2 tsp vanilla extract

CARROT DECORATION: large orange and large green gumdrops or jellied fruit slices

1 Heat oven to 375°F. Lightly grease a 12-cup mini-muffin pan (each cup should have a scant 2 Tbsp capacity).

2 In a large bowl, stir flour, sugar, baking powder, cinnamon, nutmeg, baking soda and salt until combined.

3 In a medium bowl, whisk carrots, orange juice, oil, egg and vanilla until well blended. Add all at once to flour mixture, then stir with a rubber spatula just until evenly moistened. Spoon half the batter into muffin cups. Leave remaining batter at room temperature.

4 Bake 15 to 18 minutes until a wooden pick inserted in centers comes out clean. Cool in pan on wire rack 5 minutes then remove from pan to rack to cool completely. Repeat with remaining batter.

5 ICING AND CARROT DECORATION: Mix icing ingredients

in a small bowl until smooth. Cover and refrigerate. Cut orange gumdrops into 24 carrot shapes, each about 1 in. long. Cut green gumdrops into 24 little strips. Stick onto tops of carrots.

6 UP TO 1 DAY BEFORE SERVING: Spread 1/2 tsp icing on each muffin. (Icing may weep around edges. That's normal.) Top with a carrot. Refrigerate covered until serving.

PLANNING TIP *The muffins can be stored airtight at room temperature up to 2 days or frozen up to 2 months. The decorations and icing can be made up to 2 days ahead. Refrigerate icing tightly covered; store decorations airtight at room temperature. Ice and decorate muffins up to 1 day before serving.*

Lemon Cream Tart

PASTRY SHELL

1 1/2 cups all-purpose flour
2 Tbsp sugar
1/2 stick (1/4 cup) cold butter, cut in small pieces
1/4 cup solid vegetable shortening
3 Tbsp very cold water

LEMON CREAM FILLING

3/4 cup sugar
1 Tbsp cornstarch
3 large eggs, at room temperature
1 stick (1/2 cup) butter, very soft
1/2 cup reduced-fat sour cream, at room temperature
2 1/2 Tbsp freshly grated lemon peel
1/2 cup fresh lemon juice

1 pt (12 oz) ripe strawberries, hulled and halved
    (save 1 whole berry for center)
2 ripe kiwi, peeled, halved lengthwise, then thinly sliced crosswise

1 Have ready an 11-in. tart pan with removable sides.

2 TO MAKE PASTRY SHELL IN FOOD PROCESSOR: Put
flour and sugar in food processor; pulse to mix. Add butter
and shortening; pulse just until mixture resembles small
peas. Add water all at once; pulse just until a dough forms.
Remove blade, then dough. BY HAND: Mix flour and sugar in
a medium bowl. Cut in butter and shortening with a pastry
blender until mixture resembles coarse crumbs. Sprinkle with
water, then toss with a fork until mixture clumps together.

3 Press into a 1-in.-thick disk, wrap and refrigerate 30
minutes or until firm enough to roll out.

4 On a lightly floured surface with a lightly floured
rolling pin, roll dough into a 13-in. circle. Line bottom and
sides of tart pan; cut off any excess. Place in freezer 10
minutes to firm.

5 Meanwhile heat oven to 425°F. Line pastry shell with

foil, pressing foil into corners. Bake 15 minutes, remove foil and bake 5 minutes more until top edges are lightly browned. Cool on a wire rack. Reduce oven temperature to 375°F.

6 FILLING: Meanwhile whisk sugar and cornstarch in a large bowl to combine. Whisk in eggs until combined. Whisk in butter, then sour cream, lemon peel and juice until blended (mixture will look curdled). Pour into tart shell.

7 Bake 25 to 30 minutes until set and a knife inserted near center comes out clean. Cool completely on wire rack. Cover and refrigerate at least 4 hours.

8 NO MORE THAN 4 HOURS BEFORE SERVING: Place tart pan on a small, sturdy bowl; let pan sides fall down. Place tart on a serving plate. Arrange fruit on filling as shown (see photo, opposite page). Refrigerate until serving.

Chocolate Nests

1 can (14 oz) sweetened condensed milk (not evaporated milk)
2 cups (12 oz) semisweet chocolate chips
2 cans (5 oz each) thin chow mein noodles
FILL WITH: egg-shaped Easter candies such as Jordan almonds

1 Line 2 baking sheets with foil. Lightly coat with non-stick spray.

2 Scrape condensed milk into a medium saucepan or microwave-safe bowl; add chocolate chips. Place over low heat and stir often, or microwave on high 2 to 4 minutes, stirring every minute, until chips melt and mixture is blended and smooth.

3 Put noodles into a large bowl, pour on chocolate mixture and toss with a rubber spatula until noodles are coated.

4 Drop generous 1/2 cups on prepared baking sheets. Lightly spray fingertips with nonstick spray. Form mounds into nests making a depression in the center to hold candies. Refrigerate 30 minutes or until set. Peel off foil; fill with candies.

TIME: About 20 min, plus 30 min chilling

MAKES 12

PER NEST: 369 cal, 6 g pro, 49 g car, 3 g fiber, 19 g fat (8 g saturated fat), 11 mg chol, 149 mg sod

PLANNING TIP *The nests can be made up to 3 days before serving. Store loosely covered at room temperature.*

TIME: About 1 hr (not including
baking cake layers)

SERVES 12 with extra cookies

PER SERVING (WITHOUT
COOKIES): 542 cal, 4 g pro,
77 g car, 1 g fiber, 26 g fat
(9 g saturated fat), 53 mg
chol, 369 mg sod

PLANNING TIP *The cookies can
be decorated up to 2 days
ahead. Store in a single layer,
loosely covered, at room temperature. Add to cake shortly
before serving.*

TIP *You'll have enough dough
and icing to make extra cookies
to serve on a plate at the table.*

ROYAL ICING

*In a large bowl, with mixer on
low speed, beat 1 lb confectioners' sugar and 3 Tbsp Just
Whites (powdered egg whites;
see Note, opposite page) until
well blended. Add 6 Tbsp
water and beat until well
blended. Increase mixer speed
to high and beat 8 minutes or
until icing is very thick and
white. Covered icing may be
refrigerated up to 2 weeks. If
icing separates, beat with a
spoon to blend.*

MAKES 2 1/2 cups

Easter Cake

3/4 cup all-purpose flour
1 roll (18 oz) refrigerated sugar-cookie dough
Royal Icing (see recipe, left)
*Yellow, pink, light-blue, violet and green paste or gel food color
(see Note, opposite page)*
Yellow and clear crystal (sanding) sugar
Chocolate mini-chips
2 cans (12 oz each) whipped vanilla frosting
Two round 8 x 2-in. cooled, baked cake layers, any flavor
1 1/2 cups sweetened flaked coconut
Small candy eggs and tiny candy flowers (decors)
*YOU ALSO NEED: 6 qt-size and 1 gal-size plastic ziptop bags,
at least 1 small paintbrush and a few toothpicks*

1 Heat oven to 350°F. Have ready baking sheets and
2 1/2- to 3-in. chick-shaped and 1 1/2- to 4-in. egg-shaped
cookie cutters.

2 Knead flour into cookie dough until blended. Roll
out on floured surface with floured rolling pin to scant
1/4 in. thick. Cut out chicks and assorted-size eggs with
cutters. Cut top off 1 egg in zigzags (for hatching chick).
Reroll and cut scraps. Place about 1 in. apart on
ungreased baking sheets.

3 Bake 8 to 12 minutes until golden. Transfer to a wire
rack to cool.

4 TO DECORATE COOKIES: Divide Royal Icing among 6
cups. Leaving 1 of the cups white, tint rest with food color
to desired pastel shades (colors dry slightly darker). Spoon
all the white and about 3 Tbsp of each tinted batch into qt-
size ziptop bags; press out air and seal. Cover icing in cups.

5 CHICKS: Snip tip off corner of bag with yellow icing
and pipe outline around edges of chicks, leaving some
icing in bag for wings. Add drops of water to yellow icing
in cup until consistency of honey. Dip paintbrush in icing;

fill in outlines on chicks. While wet, sprinkle with yellow sugar. Press on mini-chip eyes, flat sides up. When dry, pipe yellow swirls for wings with icing reserved in bag. Mix a little pink and yellow icing; paint beaks on chicks.

6 EGGS: Using 1 color at a time, pipe around edges and outline designs. Thin remaining icings as above; paint to fill bordered areas. Sprinkle some with clear sugar. Let set, then pipe white dots and lines on some. Place on wire racks to dry.

7 CAKE: Tint all the vanilla frosting green. Place 1 cake layer on serving plate. Spread top with 3/4 cup frosting. Top with remaining layer, bottom side up. Spread top and sides with all but 1/4 cup remaining frosting. Put about 1 tsp water and a little green food color into gal-size ziptop bag. Knead to blend. Add coconut, seal bag and shake until coconut is evenly green.

8 SHORTLY BEFORE SERVING: Press coconut around top and bottom edge of cake, reserving some. Press cookies around side of cake as shown, using reserved green frosting as glue if needed. Arrange cookies on top of cake, using toothpicks as supports. Add coconut at base of some cookies. Sprinkle with candy eggs and tiny flowers.

NOTE *Paste or gel food colors can be found in crafts, party-supply and large variety stores. Just Whites (powdered egg whites) is available in supermarkets nationwide.*

TIME: About 1 hr (includes
          baking 2 batches),
          plus 3 hr chilling
DECORATE: Depends on skill

MAKES 14

PER COOKIE: 351 cal, 4 g pro,
56 g car, 1 g fiber, 13 g fat
(7 g saturated fat), 42 mg
chol, 148 mg sod

PLANNING TIP *The dough can
be made up to 3 weeks ahead
and frozen. The cookies can be
baked and fully decorated up
to 5 days ahead. Store airtight
with wax paper between layers
at room temperature.*

TIP *To make pattern for cookies, trace outline of larger egg
(actual size printed over text,
right) on paper. Cut pattern
from cardboard.*

Big Easter Egg Cookies

DOUGH

1/2 cup toasted slivered almonds (see Toasting Nuts, page 28)
2 cups all-purpose flour
1 1/2 sticks (3/4 cup) butter, softened
1/3 cup each confectioners' sugar and packed
   light-brown sugar
1 1/2 tsp almond extract
1 tsp each vanilla extract and baking powder
1 large egg
2 Tbsp 1% lowfat milk

DECORATING ICING

1 lb confectioners' sugar
1/3 cup warm water
2 Tbsp powdered egg whites (Just Whites) or 3 Tbsp
   meringue powder (see Note, opposite page)
Green, blue, red and yellow paste (gel) food colors

DECORATION: purchased Easter icing decorations (see Note,
opposite page)

1 DOUGH: Pulse toasted almonds in a food processor
until finely chopped. Add flour; process until almonds are
finely ground.

2 Beat butter, sugars, extracts and baking powder with
mixer on medium speed until pale and fluffy. Beat in egg
until very well blended. On low speed, beat in flour mixture
and milk just until blended.

3 Divide dough in half. Form each portion into a 1-in.-
thick disk. Wrap and refrigerate 3 hours or until firm.

4 Heat oven to 350°F. Have ready baking sheet(s), a
4 1/2 x 3 1/4-in. egg-shaped cookie cutter or pattern (see
Tip) and two qt-size ziptop freezer bags, 1 fitted with a
small star piping tip.

5 On lightly floured surface with a lightly floured rolling pin, roll out 1 portion dough (keep rest refrigerated) to 1/4 in. thick. With cookie cutter or pattern, cut out eggs. Place 1 in. apart on ungreased baking sheet(s). Reroll and cut scraps only once.

6 Bake 11 to 13 minutes until bottoms and edges just start to brown. Cool on baking sheet 1 minute before removing to wire rack to cool completely. Repeat with remaining dough.

7 DECORATING ICING: Put sugar, water and powdered egg whites in a large bowl. Beat with mixer on medium speed 4 to 5 minutes or until glossy, stiff peaks form when beaters are lifted. Cover tightly until using.

8 Trace outline of smaller egg (printed within larger egg over this text, left) on paper. Cut out and place pattern about 3/4 in. from bottom edge of cookie. Faintly scratch outline of small egg with a toothpick.

9 ICE AND DECORATE: Scrape 3/4 cup icing into bag with star tip. Seal bag and cover tip until ready to use. Tint 1/4 cup icing grass-green; scrape into a ziptop bag and seal bag.

10 For each color, put a 1/2 cup icing into a custard cup. (Keep remaining icing covered.) Adding food color a little at a time, tint 1/2 cup pale blue and others to desired shade. Stir in a few drops of water until thin enough to apply with a brush or icing spatula. Spread icing to edge of cookies and near outline of smaller egg. Let set about 20 minutes. Spread pale-blue icing in small egg; let set.

11 Snip tiny corner off bag with green icing and pipe "grass." Lightly press on decorations; pipe some grass over decorations. (You can pipe your own icing pictures instead of purchased.) Using bag fitted with star tip, pipe a decorative edge around small and large egg areas. Let set.

NOTE *Just Whites is available in supermarkets nationwide. Meringue powder, paste (gel) food color and Easter icing decorations can be found in supermarket baking sections or stores selling cake-decorating supplies.*

An Easter Feast for 8

STUFFED POTATO APPETIZER

BEET SALAD ON GREENS

CRUSTED LEG OF LAMB

WILD RICE & ORZO

ROASTED SPRING VEGETABLES

ALMOND-COCONUT CREAM PIE

FRUIT & SORBET COUPE

EASTER BUNNY COOKIES

Crusted Leg of Lamb

Time: About 45 min

Makes 18 (6 of each filling)

Per potato (with Wasabi):
42 cal, 1 g pro, 1 g car, 0 g fiber, 1 g fat (0 g saturated fat), 3 mg chol, 36 mg sod
Per potato (with Curry):
35 cal, 1 g pro, 6 g car, 0 g fiber, 1 g fat (1 g saturated fat), 4 mg chol, 8 mg sod
Per potato (with Sundried Tomato): 33 cal, 1 g pro, 6 g car, 0 g fiber, 1 g fat (0 g saturated fat), 0 mg chol, 59 mg sod

PLANNING TIP *Can be prepared through Step 3 up to 2 days ahead. Refrigerate airtight.*

Stuffed Potato Appetizer

21 very small new potatoes

WASABI FILLING
   1/3 cup loosely packed parsley, finely chopped
   2 Tbsp wasabi-horseradish mayonnaise

CURRY FILLING
   3 Tbsp reduced-fat sour cream
   1 tsp lemon juice
   1/2 tsp curry powder
   Pinch of salt

SUNDRIED TOMATO FILLING
   2 Tbsp bottled sundried tomato sauce or spread

1 Cook potatoes in water to cover by 1 in. 20 minutes or until tender. Drain, dry on paper towels and refrigerate until cool.

2 Cut a thin slice off wide end of each potato so it can stand upright. Cut 18 in half crosswise, straight or zigzag. With a small spoon or melon baller, carefully scoop a hollow from both halves of potatoes into a bowl. (If you don't have 3/4 cup, use extra 3 potatoes.) Divide among 3 bowls.

3 Add Wasabi Filling to 1 bowl; mash to blend. Scrape into a ziptop bag, press out air and seal. Repeat with Curry and Sundried Tomato Fillings.

4 UP TO 2 HOURS BEFORE SERVING: Stand potato halves on platter. Snip tip off corner of bag(s); pipe fillings into hollows. Add tops.

Beet Salad on Greens

1 bunch each *(about 1 lb each)* small to medium red and golden beets, trimmed and scrubbed

DRESSING
  1/2 cup olive oil
  1/4 cup cider vinegar
  1 Tbsp grated lemon peel
  1/4 cup lemon juice
  2 Tbsp mustard
  1 Tbsp sugar
  1/2 tsp pepper
  1/4 tsp salt

1/2 cup fresh dill leaves, chopped
12 cups torn salad greens (red leaf, frisée and romaine)
1 head (7 oz) Belgian endive, cut lengthwise in strips
1 cup toasted walnuts (see Tip, page 20)

1 Heat oven to 375°F. Line a 13 x 9-in. pan with foil; coat foil with nonstick spray. Place red beets on one side; wrap golden beets in foil; place on other side. Cover pan with foil.

2 Bake 1 to 1 1/2 hours until beets are tender. When cool enough to handle, hold under running water; rub off skins and slice. Place red and golden beets in separate bowls.

3 Shake Dressing ingredients in a covered jar or whisk in a bowl to blend. Stir 1/4 cup dressing and 1/4 cup dill into each bowl of beets.

4 Mix greens, endive and nuts in a large bowl with rest of Dressing. Arrange the mixture, with beets, on salad plates or on a serving platter.

TIME: 2 hr

SERVES 8

PER SERVING: 280 cal, 5 g pro, 17 g car, 3 g fiber, 23 g fat (3 g saturated fat), 0 mg chol, 188 mg sod

PLANNING TIP *Can be prepared through Step 3 up to 1 day ahead. Cover and refrigerate.*

TIME: About 1 hr 40 min

SERVES 8

PER SERVING: 263 cal, 37 g pro,
5 g car, 0 g fiber, 9 g fat
(3 g saturated fat), 113 mg
chol, 437 mg sod

PLANNING TIP *Crust can be mixed up to 2 days ahead. Refrigerate.*

Crusted Leg of Lamb

CRUST
  1 1/2 cups fresh bread crumbs
  1 Tbsp chopped fresh rosemary or 1 tsp dried
  1 Tbsp chopped garlic
  1 Tbsp olive oil
  1/4 tsp each salt and pepper

1/2 tsp each salt and pepper
4 1/2-lb shank-half leg of lamb, trimmed of excess fat
1 1/2 Tbsp Dijon mustard

1 Place oven rack in lowest position. Heat oven to 350°F. Have ready a large roasting pan with a rack.

2 Mix Crust ingredients. Rub salt and pepper all over lamb, place on rack and spread top and sides with mustard; press Crust on mustard.

3 Roast 1 1/2 to 1 3/4 hours or until a meat thermometer inserted in thickest part of leg, not touching bone, registers 135°F (rare), 145°F (medium) or 150°F (medium-well).

4 Transfer to serving platter, cover loosely with foil to keep warm and let stand 15 minutes before carving.

Wild Rice & Orzo

1 cup each uncooked wild rice and orzo (rice-shaped pasta)
3 Tbsp butter
2 cups chopped onions
1 1/2 cups thawed frozen green peas
1/2 tsp each salt and pepper
1/3 cup sliced scallions

1 Cook wild rice and orzo separately as packages direct.

2 Meanwhile melt 1 Tbsp butter in a large nonstick skillet. Add onions; cover and cook over medium heat, stirring occasionally, 15 minutes or until tender. Stir in remaining butter, the peas, salt and pepper; cook 1 minute.

3 Drain rice and orzo; pour into serving dish. Stir in onion mixture and scallions.

TIME: About 1 hr

SERVES 8

PER SERVING: 226 cal, 8 g pro, 38 g car, 4 g fiber, 5 g fat (3 g saturated fat), 12 mg chol, 224 mg sod

Roasted Spring Vegetables

GREMOLATA
- *1/2 cup each loosely packed parsley and mint leaves, finely chopped*
- *2 tsp freshly grated lemon peel*
- *1/2 tsp each salt and minced garlic*

1 1/2 lb carrots, peeled, cut diagonally in 1/2-in. pieces
2 lb asparagus, woody ends snapped off, spears cut in half
2 Tbsp olive oil
1/2 tsp salt
1/4 tsp pepper

1 Mix Gremolata ingredients.

2 Line 2 rimmed baking sheets with foil (for easy cleanup). Place carrots on one, asparagus on the other. Toss each with 1 Tbsp oil, 1/4 tsp salt and 1/8 tsp pepper.

3 Put carrots in oven 20 minutes before lamb is done. Remove lamb and carrots from oven. Increase temperature to 450°F. Stir carrots; return to oven along with asparagus.

4 Roast 10 minutes until vegetables are browned and crisp-tender. Toss with Gremolata. Arrange on serving platter.

TIME: 50 min

SERVES 8

PER SERVING: 89 cal, 4 g pro, 12 g car, 4 g fiber, 4 g fat (1 g saturated fat), 0 mg chol, 323 mg sod

TIME: 4 hr 15 min (includes
         3 hr chilling)

SERVES 10

PER SERVING: 457 cal, 7 g pro,
  44 g car, 1 g fiber, 29 g fat
  (15 g saturated fat), 151 mg
  chol, 234 mg sod

PLANNING TIP *Prepare through
Step 4 at least 3 hours or up to
2 days ahead.*

Almond-Coconut Cream Pie

CRUST

> 30 shortbread cookies (Lorna Doone)
> 1/2 stick (1/4 cup) butter, softened

FILLING

> 3/4 cup sugar
> 5 Tbsp cornstarch
> 3 1/4 cups whole milk
> Yolks of 4 large eggs, in a medium bowl
> 2 Tbsp cold stick butter, cut up
> 3/4 cup sweetened flaked coconut
> 1 tsp vanilla extract
> 1/4 cup toasted blanched (without skin) almonds,
>   finely chopped
> 1/2 tsp almond extract
> 4 drops green food color

1 cup heavy (whipping) cream
GARNISH: Jordan almonds

1 Heat oven to 350°F. Have a 9-in. pie plate ready.

2 CRUST: Process cookies in food processor to make fine crumbs. Add butter; process to blend. Press in pie plate. Bake 10 minutes or until lightly toasted around edge. Cool on a wire rack.

3 MEANWHILE MAKE FILLING: Mix sugar and cornstarch in a medium saucepan. Whisk in milk. Place over medium heat; stir gently with whisk (if stirred too briskly Filling will be thin) until thickened and boiling (about 15 minutes), scraping bottom and corners of pan to prevent scorching. Boil 1 minute; remove from heat. Whisk 2 cups of milk mixture into yolks; stir back into saucepan. Stir over low heat 2 minutes. Remove from heat; stir in butter until melted.

4 Pour half into a medium bowl. Stir in coconut and vanilla; pour into Crust. Stir almonds, almond extract and

food color into saucepan; pour over coconut layer. Cover surface of pie with plastic wrap. Refrigerate until cool, about 3 hours.

5 To serve: Beat cream with mixer on high speed until stiff peaks form. Spread over pie; garnish with almonds.

Fruit & Sorbet Coupe

1 medium pineapple, peeled, cored and cut in chunks
16 oz strawberries, hulled and sliced
2 kiwis, peeled, cut in thin half slices
1/2 pt blueberries
1 qt raspberry-flavored ginger ale, chilled
4 pt assorted sorbets (such as raspberry, mango, passionfruit and strawberry)

Gently mix fruit in a large bowl. Refrigerate to chill, up to 4 hours. Spoon into individual dessert bowls or goblets. Slowly pour on ginger ale. Top with small scoops of sorbet.

Time: About 1 hr 20 min

Serves 8

Per serving: 364 cal, 2 g pro, 92 g car, 4 g fiber, 1 g fat (0 g saturated fat), 0 mg chol, 35 mg sod

TIME: About 2 hr (includes
1 hr chilling)

MAKES 10

PER COOKIE: 910 cal,
9 g pro, 156 g car, 1 g fiber,
29 g fat (18 g saturated fat),
117 mg chol, 148 mg sod

PLANNING TIP *Cookies can be
completed 5 days ahead. Store
airtight with wax paper between
layers at room temperature.*

Easter Bunny Cookies

DOUGH
3 sticks (1 1/2 cups) butter, softened
1 1/3 cups sugar
2 tsp vanilla extract
1 tsp nutmeg
2 large eggs
4 cups all-purpose flour
2 Tbsp freshly grated lemon peel

Icing & Decorations (see recipe, opposite page)

1 Trace outline of bunny and triangle, printed under text, on tracing paper. Enlarge 125% on photocopier. Cut out. Draw outline on heavy cardboard; cut out pattern of each.

2 COOKIES: Beat butter, sugar, vanilla, nutmeg and eggs in large bowl with mixer on medium-high speed until blended. On low speed, beat in flour. Stir in lemon peel. Divide in quarters. Pat each into a 1-in.-thick disk. Wrap separately; refrigerate at least 1 hr.

3 Heat oven to 350°F. On lightly floured wax paper with lightly floured rolling pin, roll out 1 disk to 1/4 in. thick (keep rest refrigerated).

4 Flour patterns before cutting each cookie. Place patterns on dough; cut around each with a small, sharp knife. Slide wax paper onto a baking sheet; freeze 10 minutes. Peel cookies from wax paper; place 1 in. apart on ungreased baking sheet(s). Fold down some ears for a floppy-ear effect. Save dough scraps.

5 Bake 11 to 13 minutes until cookies look dry and very pale golden at edges. Cool on baking sheet on a wire rack 1 minute before removing to rack to cool completely. Repeat with remaining dough. Gather scraps; reroll only once.

Icing & Decorations

ICING

> 3/4 cup pasteurized liquid egg whites (see Note)
> 2 lb confectioners' sugar

Black, pink, blue, green and yellow paste or gel food
colors (see Note)

*DECORATIONS: small black and small pink jelly beans
and white Tic Tacs*

1 ICING: Beat egg whites in a large bowl with mixer on
high speed until frothy. On medium speed, gradually add
sugar. Beat 5 minutes or until glossy stiff peaks form.
Remove and cover 1/4 cup.

2 Stir water, 1 Tbsp at a time, into remaining icing until
thin enough to apply without dripping.

3 To COLOR: Divide thinned icing between 6 cups.
Leaving 1 batch white, tint rest with food color to desired
shade, using a little black for pale gray trousers. Remove 2
Tbsp gray to a cup; color black for eyes. Keep tightly covered until ready to use.

4 To DECORATE: With a toothpick, lightly scratch outlines of clothing on cookies. Spread thinned white icing for
head, ears, feet and some clothing (see photo, opposite
page). Let one color dry completely before applying the
next. With thick icing, glue on jelly bean noses and Tic Tac
teeth. Draw eyes with toothpick dipped in black icing. Dip
toothpicks in tinted icing to draw details. Let dry completely.

5 Using thick icing, glue 1 long edge of a triangle cookie
to back of each bunny so it can stand on its own. Let dry
before standing cookie up.

MAKES 5 cups Icing

NOTE *Paste or gel food colors
can be found in crafts, party-
supply and large variety stores.
Just Whites (powdered egg
whites) is available in supermarkets nationwide.*

Valentine Hearts

1/3 cup uncooked oats, quick or old-fashioned
1 roll (18 oz) refrigerated sugar-cookie dough
DECORATION: 3 1/2 x 2 3/4-in. heart-shaped cookie cutter;
  Royal Icing (see recipe, right); pink, yellow, orange, green
  and violet paste or gel food color (see Note, page 101);
  and 5 disposable decorating bags fitted with plain,
  round writing tip(s) (see Tip)

1 Heat oven to 350°F. Have baking sheet(s) ready.

2 Process oats in a blender or food processor until finely ground. Put cookie dough into a medium bowl; add oats and knead until blended.

3 Roll out dough with a lightly floured rolling pin on a lightly floured surface to 1/4 in. thick. Cut out hearts with cutter dipped in flour. Place 2 in. apart on ungreased baking sheet(s). Reroll and cut scraps.

4 Bake 7 to 9 minutes until golden. Remove to a wire rack to cool.

5 TO DECORATE: For white and each color, put Royal Icing into small bowls or cups. Stir in food color (cover airtight when not using). Put about half of each into a smaller bowl or paper cup and stir in water, a few drops at a time, until icing is thin enough to spread. Spread a thin layer on each cookie. Let icing dry at least 30 minutes before writing messages.

6 Spoon unthinned icings into bags fitted with writing tips and pipe a message on each cookie. Let icing dry at least 20 minutes.

TIME: 33 min (includes baking 2 batches)
DECORATE: Depends on skill

MAKES 16

PER 2 COOKIES: 495 cal, 3 g pro, 97 g car, 0 g fiber, 10 g fat (3 g saturated fat), 20 mg chol, 236 mg sod

PLANNING TIP *Store iced cookies airtight with wax paper between layers at cool room temperature up to 1 week.*

ROYAL ICING

In a large bowl, with mixer on low speed, beat 1 lb confectioners' sugar and 3 Tbsp Just Whites (powdered egg whites) until well blended. Add 6 Tbsp water and beat until well blended. Increase mixer speed to high and beat 8 minutes or until icing is very thick and white. Covered icing may be refrigerated up to 2 weeks. If icing separates, beat with a spoon to blend.

MAKES 2 1/2 cups

TIP *If your pastry bags are fitted with couplers, you need only 1 piping tip. Switch the tip from color to color, washing tip clean between each.*

TIME: About 55 min
        (includes making
        frosting)
DECORATE: Depends on skill

SERVES 12

PER SERVING (without
   decoration): 467 cal, 5 g pro,
   61 g car, o g fiber, 28 g fat
   (14 g saturated fat),
   77 mg chol, 224 mg sod

PLANNING TIP *Can be made
through Step 6 up to 4 days
ahead. Refrigerate loosely covered. Decorate up to 1 day
before serving.*

NOTE *Paste or gel food colors
can be found in crafts, party-
supply and large variety stores.
Air Heads candy bars can be
found at candy counters and in
supermarkets. If too hard to
roll out easily, warm them
briefly in microwave.*

Sweetheart Cake

2/3 cup water

1 cup mixed golden raisins and dried cherries (such as Sun Maid), coarsely chopped

1/4 cup light rum or apple juice

1 box (18.25 oz) white cake mix

3 large eggs

1 cup reduced-fat sour cream

1/2 cup vegetable oil

Rum Frosting (see recipe, opposite page)

DECORATION: red paste or gel food color (see Note); qt-size ziptop freezer bag; 3 3/4 x 3-in., 2 1/2 x 2-in. and 1 1/4 x 1-in. heart-shaped cookie cutters (often sold as a set); 4 cherry Air Heads bars; red crystal sugar; tiny candy hearts

1 Bring water to a boil in a medium saucepan. Add raisins and cherries, reduce heat and simmer uncovered 4 minutes or until liquid is almost absorbed. Remove from heat; stir in rum. Let cool.

2 Heat oven to 350°F. Grease two 9 x 2-in. round cake pans. Line bottoms with wax paper; grease paper.

3 In a large bowl, beat cake mix, eggs, sour cream and oil with mixer on low speed 1 minute until blended. Increase mixer speed to medium; beat 2 minutes or until thickened. Fold in fruit mixture. Spread batter in prepared pans.

4 Bake 28 minutes or until a wooden pick inserted in centers comes out clean. Cool in pans on a wire rack 10 minutes. Invert on rack; peel off paper; cool completely.

5 Prepare Rum Frosting (see recipe, opposite page). Remove 1/2 cup to a bowl, tint red and scrape into ziptop bag. Seal bag and reserve.

6 Place one cake layer smooth side up on a serving platter. Spread top with 1/2 cup untinted frosting. Top with other layer, smooth side up. Frost top and sides with remaining untinted frosting.

7 UP TO 1 DAY BEFORE SERVING: Wrap rolling pin with

Melt 6 oz white baking chocolate as package directs. Scrape into a large bowl and stir in 2 Tbsp light rum or apple juice. Add 2 sticks (1 cup) softened unsalted butter and 1/3 cup reduced-fat sour cream. Beat with mixer until blended. Add 2 1/2 cups confectioners' sugar; beat 3 minutes until thick, fluffy and white.

plastic wrap. Place Air Heads side by side, slightly overlapping, on work surface. Roll out (see Note) until smooth and merged into each other. Using cookie cutters, cut out four 2 1/2 x 2-in. and eight 1 1/4 x 1-in. hearts. Reroll and cut scraps as needed. Cut a 1 1/4 x 1-in. heart from the middle of a 2 1/2 x 2-in. heart.

8 Place hearts on cake (see photo, above). Put 3 3/4 x 3-in. cookie cutter over each 2 1/2 x 2-in. heart (except heart with cutout); sprinkle red sugar on frosting around heart but inside cutter. Lift cutter straight up. Sprinkle red sugar in center of cutout heart. Place candy hearts on top and sides of cake.

9 Snip tip off 1 corner of ziptop bag. Pipe dots around bottom edge and top and sides of cake. Refrigerate cake until about 2 hours before serving.

TIME: 1 hr 40 min
DECORATE: Depends on skill

SERVES 16

PER SERVING (without
decoration): 471 cal, 5 g pro,
67 g car, 1 g fiber, 21 g fat
(12 g saturated fat), 80 mg
chol, 313 mg sod

PLANNING TIP *Can be made
up to 2 days ahead. Refrigerate
in a cake keeper or covered
with a large bowl.*

NOTE *Paste or gel food colors
can be found in crafts, party-
supply and large variety stores.*

Red Velvet Cake

1 1/2 sticks (3/4 cup) butter, softened
1 1/2 cups sugar
1 Tbsp unsweetened cocoa powder
1 1/2 tsp each baking soda and vanilla extract
2 large eggs
1 cup reduced-fat sour cream
2 Tbsp (1 oz) liquid red food color or 2 tsp red paste or gel
   food color (see Note)
4 tsp distilled white vinegar
3 cups flour

BUTTERCREAM FROSTING
   1 1/2 sticks (3/4 cup) butter, softened
   1 lb confectioners' sugar
   1/3 cup reduced-fat sour cream
   1 tsp vanilla extract
   Red liquid or red paste or gel food color

DECORATION: disposable pastry bag fitted with a plain tip with 1/2-in. opening, tiny candy heart decors, white crystal sugar

1 Heat oven to 350°F. Lightly grease and flour a 9-in. (7-cup capacity) heart-shaped cake pan.

2 CAKE: In a large bowl with mixer on high speed, beat butter, sugar, cocoa powder, baking soda and vanilla until creamy. Beat in eggs until well blended.

3 With mixer on low speed, beat in sour cream, food color and vinegar. Add flour and beat just until blended. Spread evenly in prepared pan.

4 Bake 1 hour or until a toothpick inserted in center comes out clean (cake will have a cracked hump; that's OK). Cool in pan on wire rack 10 minutes, then invert cake on rack, turning top side up and cooling completely.

5 BUTTERCREAM FROSTING: In a medium bowl with mixer on high speed, beat butter until creamy. Add sugar, sour cream and vanilla. Beat on medium-low speed until blended; increase speed to high and beat until smooth and fluffy. Tint frosting pink with red food color. Makes 3 1/2 cups.

6 Cut cake into 2 layers with a serrated knife. Place bottom layer on serving plate. Put 1 cup frosting in a cup. Spread a generous 1/3 cup in center of layer to about 1 in. from edge. Scrape frosting remaining in cup into decorating bag and pipe a border around edge of cake. Top with other cake layer, hump side up. Pipe remaining frosting on cake (see directions, right), or spread in swirls. Sprinkle with hearts and crystal sugar.

TIP This batter can also be used to make 24 cupcakes. Bake them 20 to 25 minutes.

TO PIPE FROSTING

Have point of heart facing away from you. Starting at point, pipe along right side of heart to top middle of heart as follows: Hold bag of frosting at a 45-degree angle close to surface of cake, end of bag pointing right. Squeeze and slightly lift tip as icing builds and fans out. Relax pressure as you pull bag down to the right to make a tail. Stop squeezing; pull tip away. Start each new bead slightly behind tail of previous shell. Repeat on left side of heart. Continue piping alternate sides to the middle.

TIME: About 3 hr (includes 2 hr chilling and baking 4 batches)

MAKES 128 little (1 1/2 in.) cookies

PER 4 COOKIES (without decorating sugar): 81 cal, 1 g pro, 9 g car, 0 g fiber, 5 g fat (3 g saturated fat), 18 mg chol, 46 mg sod

PLANNING TIP *The dough can be prepared through Step 4 up to 3 months ahead and frozen (let thaw at room temperature 10 minutes or until easy to slice). Decorated cookies can be stored with wax paper between layers in an airtight container at room temperature up to 1 week.*

TIP *For a sharper point on bottom of each heart, slightly pinch the dough.*

Quick-Cut Heart Cookies

1 1/2 sticks (3/4 cup) butter
1/2 cup sugar
1 large egg
1/2 tsp vanilla extract
2 cups all-purpose flour
TO DECORATE: assorted colors decorating (crystal) sugar
YOU ALSO NEED: two 8 1/2 x 11-in. sheets cardboard, bottom of 1 egg carton, one 12-in. or longer wooden skewer

1 TO PREPARE HOLDERS FOR DOUGH ROPES: Cut cardboard sheets in half lengthwise; fold all 4 pieces in half lengthwise. Place in inverted egg carton (see photo, left).

2 DOUGH: Beat butter, sugar, egg and vanilla with mixer on medium-high speed until fluffy. Reduce speed to low; beat in flour just until blended.

3 Moisten work surface; top with a square piece of plastic wrap. Divide dough in quarters. Place 1 portion on the plastic wrap; roll into an 8-in.-long rope. Set rope of dough, still on plastic wrap, into one cardboard holder. Rope will gradually conform to a point at V of cardboard. Center skewer lengthwise on rope, press skewer about halfway through dough, remove skewer and shape both sides into top of heart. Overlap wrap to cover dough. Repeat with remaining dough.

4 Leaving wrapped ropes on carton, freeze 2 hours or refrigerate overnight until dough is firm enough to slice neatly.

5 Heat oven to 350°F. Have baking sheet(s) ready.

6 Cut 1 rope at a time (leave rest refrigerated) into 1/4-in.-thick hearts (see Tip). Dip 1 side in colored sugar. Place 1/2 in. apart on ungreased baking sheet. Bake 8 to 9 minutes or until lightly brown around edges. Remove to countertop to cool.

Individual Tiramisu

12 Italian savoiardi ladyfingers (see FYI)
1/4 cup brewed cold espresso or strong coffee
1/4 cup Kahlúa (coffee-flavored liqueur)
1 tub (8 oz) mascarpone cheese
3 Tbsp sugar
1 Tbsp milk
1 tsp vanilla extract
1/2 cup heavy (whipping) cream
3 Tbsp finely chopped semisweet chocolate
TO DECORATE: tiny candy hearts and mint sprigs
YOU ALSO NEED: a decorating bag fitted with a small
  star piping tip (see Note)

1 Place ladyfingers on a rimmed baking sheet or tray. Mix espresso and Kahlúa and brush on both sides of ladyfingers to moisten. Cover with plastic wrap and refrigerate at least 2 hours or overnight.

2 Stir mascarpone, sugar, milk and vanilla in a medium bowl until blended.

3 Beat cream in a large bowl with mixer on high speed until soft peaks form when beaters are lifted. Fold into cheese mixture. Cover and refrigerate at least 2 hours.

4 UP TO 1 HOUR BEFORE SERVING: Cut ladyfingers in half diagonally (see diagram A, right). Place a top half on each dessert plate. Flip bottom half over and place next to top half to form a heart (see diagram B). Spoon cheese mixture into decorating bag. Pipe on hearts, sprinkle each with 1 1/2 tsp chopped chocolate, then top with another ladyfinger. Pipe on remaining mascarpone mixture. Decorate with candy hearts and mint. Refrigerate until serving.

TIME: 2 hr 50 min (includes 2 hr setting)

SERVES 6

PER SERVING: 384 cal, 5 g pro, 29 g car, 0 g fiber, 26 g fat (17 g saturated fat), 59 mg chol, 75 mg sod

PLANNING TIP *Prepare through Step 3 at least 2 hours or up to 1 day ahead. Can be assembled (Step 4) up to 1 hour ahead.*

FYI *Imported Italian savoiardi ladyfingers are crisp and longer than the familiar soft sponge-cake variety.*

NOTE *Piping tips can be found in some supermarkets or stores selling crafts, party or cake decorating supplies.*

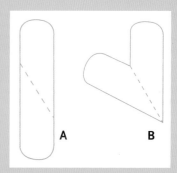

A   B

TIME: Depends on skill

SERVES 12

PER SERVING: 441 cal,
  7 g pro, 69 g car, 3 g fiber,
  16 g fat (8 g saturated fat),
  22 mg chol, 455 mg sod

I Scream for Witches

2 pt green mint chocolate chip ice cream
1/2 cup semisweet chocolate chips, melted
HATS: 12 chocolate ice cream cones, 12 chocolate wafer cookies
  and red licorice lace
EYES: sprinkle decors, mini-baking bits (M&M's)
NOSES: 12 bugle-shaped crispy corn snacks
HAIR: shredded wheat cereal
12 chocolate cream-filled cupcakes

1 Freeze 12 scoops of the ice cream on a baking sheet.

2 HATS: Use melted chocolate to glue rims of cones to cookies. When set, tie licorice lace around hats. EYES: Glue decor irises on baking bits.

3 Working with 2 scoops ice cream at a time, press on hats, noses, eyes and hair. Return to freezer.

4 TO SERVE: Set witches on cupcakes.

Fossil Pops

12 lollipop sticks (see Note, opposite page)
12 gummy worms, dinosaurs or Swedish fish gummy candies
2 cups sugar
3/4 cup light corn syrup
3/4 cup water
1/4 to 2 tsp flavoring extract or flavoring oil (see Note, opposite
  page), depending on intensity of flavor
Red and yellow liquid food color

1 Lightly oil 2 large baking sheets. Place on wire cooling racks. Arrange 6 sticks on each so syrup won't touch or drip over edge when poured. Put a gummy candy on top of each.

2 Stir sugar, corn syrup and water in a saucepan over medium-high heat just until sugar dissolves.

3 Without stirring, boil until candy thermometer regis-

TIME: Depends on skill

MAKES 12

PER SERVING: 219 cal,
  o g pro, 56 g car, o g fiber,
  o g fat (o g saturated fat),
  o mg chol, 26 mg sod

TIP *Keep children away from the very hot syrup.*

NOTE *Flavoring oils and lolli-pop sticks are available at baking-supply shops and party-supply and crafts stores.*

ters 300°F to 310°F. Immediately remove from heat and wait just until boiling stops. Stir in extract or oil (you'll need more extract than oil) and a drop of each color.

4 Working quickly, spoon 2 to 3 Tbsp syrup to cover upper 1/4 of sticks and the candies. (Lollipops will have odd shapes and candies may melt slightly, but will firm as pops cool.) Cool completely, then gently slide pops off cookie sheet. Wrap individually in plastic wrap (wax paper will stick).

TIME: 50 min
DECORATE: Depends on skill

SERVES 12

PER SERVING (without spider):
569 cal, 12 g pro, 65 g car,
3 g fiber, 31 g fat (13 g saturated
fat), 88 mg chol, 410 mg sod

Peanut Butter Spiderweb Cake

PEANUT BUTTER CAKE
1 cup creamy peanut butter
1/4 cup butter, softened
1 1/2 cups sugar
1 Tbsp baking powder
1 Tbsp vanilla extract
3/4 tsp baking soda
3 large eggs
1 1/2 cups buttermilk
2 1/4 cups flour

CHOCOLATE GLAZE
3/4 cup heavy cream
1 1/2 cups semisweet chocolate chips

SPIDERWEB
2 Tbsp each sugar, creamy peanut butter and heavy cream
Red and yellow liquid food color

SPIDER: 2 Tbsp shredded coconut, red and yellow liquid food color, 1 chocolate-covered marshmallow cookie (Mallomar), 1/4 cup semisweet chocolate chips (melted), mini-baking bits (M&M's), green jelly bean, green gummy straws

1 Heat oven to 350°F. Lightly grease two 8 or 9 x 2-in. round cake pans.

2 CAKE: Beat peanut butter and butter in large bowl on high until smooth. Beat in sugar, baking powder, vanilla and baking soda to blend. Mixture will be thick and crumbly. Beat in eggs, 1 at a time, until well blended and batter is pale. On low speed, beat in buttermilk. When blended, gradually add flour and beat just until blended. Divide evenly between pans.

3 Bake 35 to 40 minutes until a pick inserted near centers comes out clean. Cool in pans on wire rack 10

minutes, then invert pans, tap to release cakes and cool completely.

4 CHOCOLATE GLAZE: Heat cream until steaming hot. Off heat, add chocolate. Let stand 1 to 2 minutes. Stir until smooth. Let cool 20 to 30 minutes until slightly thickened, but pourable.

5 SPIDERWEB: Heat sugar, peanut butter and cream until steaming hot. Off heat, stir until smooth. Tint orange with red and yellow food color. Cool 20 minutes until slightly thickened, but pourable.

6 MEANWHILE ASSEMBLE CAKE: Place 1 layer upside down on serving plate. Pour on and spread 1/2 the Glaze, letting some drip down sides. Top with second layer right side up. Repeat with remaining Glaze.

7 Pour Spiderweb mixture into an unpleated ziptop sandwich bag and seal. Snip off tip of corner and pipe 4 circles on cake and a quarter-size spot in center. Immediately drag a toothpick through circles 8 times from center of cake to edges.

8 SPIDER: In plastic bag, toss coconut with drops of food color until orange. Coat cookie with chocolate, then coconut. Press on baking-bits eyes. Halve jelly bean; press in place for pincers. Place gummy straws on cake for legs. Set spider body on legs. Cover and refrigerate up to 5 days.

TIME: Depends on skill

MAKES 8

PER SERVING: 818 cal,
 5 g pro, 124 g car, 1 g fiber,
 34 g fat (13 g saturated fat),
 64 mg chol, 450 mg sod

PLANNING TIP *May be made up to 8 hours before serving. Leave at room temperature.*

NOTE *Paste or gel food colors can be found in crafts, party-supply and large variety stores.*

Mini Haunted Houses

1 frozen family-size (16 oz) poundcake, thawed
2 tubs (16 oz each) vanilla frosting
Orange paste or gel food color (see Note)
32 chocolate wafer cookies (from a 9-oz pkg), crushed
WALKWAYS: 8 creme-filled sugar wafers
ROOFS: thin pretzel sticks
DOORS: 8 Necco candy wafers
WINDOWS: 8 pieces Froot Loops cereal
GHOSTS: 8 bugle-shaped crispy corn snacks
8 purchased tiny candy pumpkins

1 Place wax paper on cutting board. Place cake on wax paper. Cut 1/4 in. off both ends of cake. Starting 1 in. from top of left side of cake, cut cake in half diagonally to 1 in. from bottom edge of right side (see Cooking Lesson A, opposite page). Turn each half so sides of cake are on the wax paper. Cut off thin brown crust.

2 Put 1/2 cup vanilla frosting in a cup; cover and reserve. Color remaining frosting orange. Spread some frosting under cake halves and place a rounded tsp in center of 8 dessert plates.

3 Using 1 2/3 cups orange frosting, frost diagonally cut side (see Cooking Lesson B, opposite page), then frost rest of cake except ends.

4 Cut each cake crosswise in quarters to make 8 houses. Set a house into frosting on each plate. Use remaining orange frosting to frost cut sides. Sprinkle crushed wafers around each house.

5 WALKWAYS: Remove top cookie layer of sugar wafers. Place a wafer creme side up on each plate, breaking off an end if needed to fit.

6 ROOFS: Break pretzel sticks into assorted lengths and press into frosting on roofs. DOORS: Break candy wafers in half. Press into frosting. WINDOWS: Press Froot Loops into frosting.

7 GHOSTS: Gently dip corn snacks, one at a time, into reserved vanilla frosting, twisting to swirl the frosting. Set 1 ghost and 1 candy pumpkin on each plate. Use crumbs on plate for ghost's eyes.

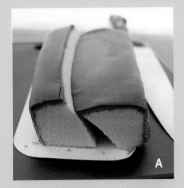

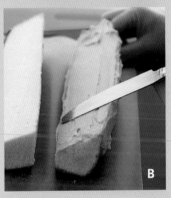

COOKING LESSON

A. *Starting 1 in. from top of left side of cake, cut cake in half diagonally to 1 in. from bottom edge of right side.*

B. *Turn each half so sides of cake are on the wax paper, diagonally cut sides up. Cut off thin brown crust. Frost diagonally cut sides first, or cake will topple over.*

Pumpkin Cheesecake Mousse Pie

One 6-oz ready-to-fill chocolate crumb crust (reserve plastic lid)
1 cup canned pumpkin
1/2 cup heavy (whipping) cream
2 cups confectioners' sugar
1 tsp vanilla extract
2 bricks (8 oz each) cream cheese (not whipped or reduced-fat),
  softened
1/2 tsp ground cinnamon
1/4 tsp each ground ginger and nutmeg

1 Refrigerate crust until ready to fill.

2 Drain pumpkin in a strainer lined with 3 layers paper towels 1 hour, stirring often.

3 Beat cream, 1/4 cup sugar and vanilla with mixer on medium-high speed until stiff peaks form when beaters are lifted.

4 In another bowl (no need to wash beaters), beat 8 oz cream cheese and 3/4 cup sugar until fluffy. Beat in 1/4 cup cream mixture, then fold in rest until well mixed. Spread in chilled crust and refrigerate.

5 In same bowl, beat remaining cream cheese and sugar, and the spices. When smooth, beat in pumpkin until blended. Spoon on white layer, then spread evenly. Cover with lid; refrigerate overnight or up to 3 days.

TIME: 20 min, plus
        overnight chilling

SERVES 12

PER SERVING: 327 cal, 4 g pro, 32 g car, 1 g fiber, 20 g fat (11 g saturated fat), 55 mg chol, 184 mg sod

PREP: 1 hr 55 min
DECORATE: Depends on skill

SERVES 20

PER SERVING: 633 cal,
  5 g pro, 106 g car, 0 g fiber,
  23 g fat (6 g saturated fat),
  64 mg chol, 409 mg sod

MARSHMALLOW DOUGH

1 tub or jar (7 or 7 1/2 oz)
   marshmallow cream (such
   as Marshmallow Fluff
   or Creme)
2 3/4 to 3 1/4 cups
   confectioners' sugar

Scrape marshmallow cream
into a large bowl. Stir in as
much sugar as possible, then
knead in remaining sugar until
a smooth dough forms. (Dough
should be stiff yet pliable.)
Wrap airtight in plastic wrap
until ready to use. Store at
room temperature.

PLANNING TIP Keeps well up
to 1 week.

NOTE Paste or gel food colors
can be found in crafts, party-
supply and large variety stores.

Jack-o'-Lantern Cake

2 boxes (18.5 oz each) cake mix, any flavor
2 cans (16 oz each) vanilla frosting
Orange, yellow and green paste or gel food color (see Note)
Marshmallow Dough (see recipe, left)
1/2 cup canned dark-chocolate frosting

1 Place oven rack in middle position. Heat to 350°F. Grease and flour a 6-cup bundt pan and one 8 x 2-in. round cake pan. Have ready a leaf-shaped cookie cutter.

2 Prepare cake mix as package directs. Fill 8-in. cake pan and bundt pan with 3 cups batter each (cover and leave remaining batter at room temperature).

3 Bake both cakes on middle rack 35 to 40 minutes or until a wooden pick inserted in centers of cakes comes out clean. Cool cakes in pans on wire racks 15 minutes, then invert cakes on racks to cool completely.

4 Wash, grease and flour the 6-cup bundt pan. Add remaining batter; bake and cool as above.

5 If necessary, trim rounded bottoms (humps) off bundt cakes and top of round cake with a long serrated knife until flat, saving any scraps. Brush off crumbs.

6 Tint vanilla frosting orange. Remove 1 cup and add more orange food color to it for a darker orange.

7 TO ASSEMBLE: Place 1 bundt cake flat side up on a serving plate. Spread top with a thin layer of lighter orange frosting. Set round cake on top, trimming to fit and saving the scraps. Thinly frost top and place other bundt cake on top, lining up ridges of top bundt cake with ridges of bottom bundt cake. Place scraps in hole in center (to support stem added later). Spread cakes with a thin layer of lighter orange frosting. Refrigerate 15 minutes.

8 Using vertical strokes, spread the remaining lighter

orange frosting on pumpkin, making pumpkin-like ridges from top to bottom.

9 Spoon darker orange frosting into a qt-size ziptop bag; seal bag, then cut off a tiny corner. Pipe lines, about 2 in. apart, from top to bottom of pumpkin, then drag back of a teaspoon through the lines to create ridges and blend darker and lighter oranges.

10 Place 1/2 the Marshmallow Dough (see recipe, opposite page) on work surface lightly dusted with cornstarch. Knead in yellow food color. Tint remaining dough green (for a variegated look, tint some a darker green, then knead both greens together until marbled but not completely blended); wrap in plastic wrap.

11 With rolling pin and work surface lightly dusted with cornstarch, roll out yellow dough to a scant 1/4 in. thick (the dough dries easily, so work quickly). Following photo, right, cut out eyes, nose and mouth, rerolling scraps. Press in place on pumpkin, using a dab of water to adhere if needed. Roll about half the green dough into a cylinder for the pumpkin stem. Insert in hole in pumpkin at a rakish angle. Roll out remaining green dough and cut out leaves. Roll scraps into tendrils. Place around stem.

12 Spoon chocolate frosting into a qt-size ziptop bag; seal bag, then cut off a tiny corner. Pipe outline around eyes, nose and mouth.

TIME: About 1 hr

MAKES 8

PER APPLE (without decoration):
537 cal, 0 g pro,
140 g car, 3 g fiber, 1 g fat
(0 g saturated fat),
0 mg chol, 66 mg sod

PLANNING TIP *Can be made up to 1 day ahead. Store uncovered at room temperature.*

NOTE *If you don't have a candy thermometer, start checking the temperature of the syrup after it's been boiling about 25 minutes using the ice water test described in Step 5.*

Candied Halloween Apples

8 Golden Delicious apples
8 ice cream sticks
1 each red, green and blue Fruit Roll-Ups
3 cups sugar
1 1/4 cups each light corn syrup and water
Red and yellow liquid food color or orange paste or gel food color (see Note, page 120)

1 Line a baking sheet with foil; coat with nonstick spray.

2 Wash apples; dry thoroughly with paper towels. Remove stems. Insert sticks into stem end of apples.

3 Cut faces or spiderwebs from Fruit Roll-Ups; press them onto the apples.

4 Put the sugar, corn syrup and water in a 2-qt saucepan over medium heat just until sugar dissolves. Cover pan and boil 3 minutes. Uncover pan, carefully attach a candy thermometer to side (see Note) and, without stirring, increase heat to medium-high.

5 Continue to boil and, without stirring, boil 30 minutes or until candy thermometer registers 300°F to 310°F. (Or drop a small amount of syrup from tip of a spoon into ice water. When mixture forms a brittle mass that snaps easily when pressed between fingers, it's ready.) Immediately remove from heat; wait until boiling stops. Take great care, the syrup is extremely hot.

6 Stir in food color until thoroughly blended. Tipping saucepan slightly so the syrup is deeper on one side, immerse 1 of the apples. Twirl it a few times to coat completely, then remove from syrup and twirl a few more times letting excess syrup fall back into saucepan.

7 Lightly drag base of apple over lip of the saucepan to remove additional syrup. Set apple on sprayed foil. Working quickly, coat rest of apples with remaining syrup.

TIME: 10 min, plus overnight freezing

MAKES about 15 cups

PER CUP (without bats):
160 cal, 1 g pro, 39 g car, 0 g fiber, 1 g fat (1 g saturated fat), 3 mg chol, 44 mg sod

PLANNING TIP *The ice bats can be made up to 2 weeks ahead. Remove from molds and freeze in a ziptop bag.*

TIP *Candy molds are available where candy and cake decorating supplies are sold.*

Dracula's Punch

About 1 cup purple grape juice
6 cups cran-strawberry juice, chilled
6 cups raspberry ginger ale, chilled
1 tub (1 qt) rainbow sherbet

1 Have ready 2 sheets of candy bat molds with 2 bat molds on each (see Tip) and a large punch bowl. Secure bat molds on a baking sheet with foil to keep them from tipping. Carefully pour grape juice into molds; freeze.

2 To SERVE: Pour cran-strawberry juice and ginger ale into punch bowl. Spoon sherbet into bowl; stir to mix. Place frozen bats on top.

Index

(Page numbers in *italic* refer to illustrations.)

Photo credits

Cover: Alison Miksch; pp. 8, 11, 12, 17, 19, 20, 23: Tom McWilliam; pp. 26, 29, 31, 37, 39, 41, 43: Alison Miksch; pp. 46, 49, 51, 52, 56: Charles Schiller; pp. 57, 59, 61: Jacqueline Hopkins; pp. 62, 64, 65, 66, 67, 68, 69, 71, 73, 74, 77: Charles Schiller; pp. 78, 80, 81, 83, 85, 86, 87, 89, 91: Jacqueline Hopkins; pp. 92, 94, 95, 96, 97, 98, 99, 100: Dasha Wright; p. 102: Tom McWilliam; p. 105: John Uher; p. 106: Jacqueline Hopkins; pp. 109, 110: Charles Schiller; pp. 113, 115: Tony Cenicola; p. 117: Jacqueline Hopkins; p. 118: John Uher; p. 121: Tom McWilliam; pp. 122, 123: Dasha Wright. Back cover (clockwise from top left): Charles Schiller, Jacqueline Hopkins, John Uher, Charles Schiller.

Acknowledgments

The publisher wishes to thank Jane Chesnutt; Ellen R. Greene, Nancy dell'Aria, Mary Ellen Banashek, Marisol Vera, Terry Grieco Kenny, Christine Makuch and Susan Kadel; Sue Kakstys, Michele Fedele, Robb Riedel, Kim Walker, Greg Robertson, Margaret T. Farley; Cathy Dorsey; and all the photographers whose images are reproduced in the book.

Recipes and food styling by Nancy Dell'Aria, Terry Grieco Kenny, Christine Makuch and Susan Kadel.